PRACTICAL CONTRACT & COMMERCIAL NEGOTIATIONS

RAY CARTER
KENNY CAMPBELL

ISBN 10: 1903-499-97-6
ISBN 13: 978-1903-499-97-9

The contents of this publication are provided in good faith and neither The Author nor The Publisher can be held responsible for any errors or omissions contained herein. Any person relying upon the information must independently satisfy himself or herself as to the safety or any other implications of acting upon such information and no liability shall be accepted either by The Author or The Publisher in the event of reliance upon such information nor for any damage or injury arising from any interpretation of its contents. This publication may not be used in any process of risk assessment.

Printed and bound in the United Kingdom by 4edge Ltd, 22 Eldon Way Industrial Estate, Hockley, Essex, SS5 4AD.

Contents

Foreword

Within business, negotiation skills are prized and large amounts are spent on training. Yet in many cases negotiation does not generate anticipated benefits. Today's volatile and uncertain markets demand greater agility and flexibility, which can be achieved only through more collaborative relationships and radically different approaches to negotiation.

Research by the International Association of Contract and Commercial Managers (IACCM) suggests that more than 90% of negotiated agreements do not result in a win-win outcome and yet true negotiation is necessarily about working out a deal that will be right for the long-term commercial interests of the parties.

The importance of effective negotiation has never been greater. The 21st century has seen an explosion of long-term service-based arrangements. Increasingly effective negotiators are taking actions to transform their approach. The most successful are those that are targeted on eliminating the causes of negotiations being adversarial. IACCM's prescriptions re-focus negotiation as a process that brings partners together to build powerful collaborations that deliver value for both parties over the long term.

This book offers practitioners a practical guide and useful insights to the basics of effective contract and commercial negotiations, whatever point in the contracting lifecycle they occur. It is therefore invaluable for the individual professional who wishes to build their personal negotiation skills, knowledge and capabilities.

It is time to make win-win a reality.

Sally Hughes, CEO
International Association of Contract and Commercial Managers

CHAPTER 1 | INTRODUCTION TO PRACTICAL CONTRACT AND COMMERCIAL NEGOTIATIONS

Definitions

The definition we have created for this key activity is:

'Commercial negotiation is a process whereby two or more commercial parties attempt to persuade each other to accept the merits of their relative bargaining and positions and to influence each other to reconcile their often-competing needs'.

There are many other definitions regarding what is meant by the act of commercial negotiation, these include:

- "A process designed to reconcile two or more different opinions in order that appropriate actions may be initiated or continued in mutually satisfying conditions"
- "Negotiation is any form of communication in which the participant seeks to exploit relative strength of their position."
- "A formal process that occurs when parties are trying to find a mutually acceptable solution."

A commercial negotiation is an interactive communication process that may take place whenever we want something from someone else or another person wants something from us.

The Chartered Institute of Purchasing and Supply (CIPS) states that, "Negotiation starts from the first communication between the buyer and the supplier right through to the final signing of the contract. Negotiation is used to obtain a discount, agree timescales for a launch, and come to an agreement on contract terms for complex purchases. It is the buyer's responsibility to negotiate the best terms, conditions and price for every purchase whilst maintaining or improving quality or service".

Negotiation is a process whereby two persons or groups strive to reach agreement on issues or courses of action where there is some degree of difference in interest, goals, values or beliefs. The job of the negotiator is to build credibility with the "other side " find some common ground (shared interests), learn the opposing position, and share information that will persuade the "other side" to agree to a particular desired outcome.

The International Association for Contract & Commercial Management (IACCM) defines the purpose of a negotiated contract is to "Enable the creation and delivery of value for both sides, we must keep this objective at the front of our minds throughout the planning, preparation and the negotiation itself".

These popular definitions have several things in common, firstly they recognise that commercial negotiation is a process, which means there are definite stages in the commercial negotiation process, starting with planning and preparation. Next, they highlight the desire for a sustainable or mutually acceptable outcome. The imposition of one parties needs and objectives on the other is not a commercial negotiation. These definitions also refer to the need for communication between the parties.

Art or Science?

Negotiation if often described as both a science and an art. It is a science because the techniques and models can be used systematically to generate a result. It is an art when the negotiator explores the implications of the answers. Yet commercial negotiation is also a skill that can be learned and developed via training and experience. These skills require practice to be perfected. The ability to negotiate effectively is a core competence for all commercial managers.

The 5 Ps of Effective Negotiations

We have developed a simple checklist of the requirements for an effective negotiated outcome framed around these Five Ps:

- Planning for the negotiations, including aims objectives strategies and tactics.
- Prepare for the negotiations, including market conditions, relative bargaining positions, SWOT and participant profiles.
- Participate in the negotiations, including influencing and persuading skills
- Perform in the negotiations and achieve the aims and objectives.
- Post negotiation analysis including the benefits gained and the impact upon the relationship with the supplier.

When Not to Negotiate?

There are some situations and circumstances where commercial negotiation is either not possible or there is no real value to be added. These include:

- Low value goods or services – whereby the cost of commercial negotiation would not be out weight by the benefits derived.
- Branded items – whereby the supplier has a semi monopolistic control of the market.
- Regulated Markets – in many public-sector organisations in countries which have signed up the WTO (General Procurement Agreement GPA) direct commercial negotiation with suppliers are discouraged and there is heavy reliance on open and transparent competition via a formal tender and bid methodology.

Robert Mnookin of the Harvard Business School states "We must thoroughly analyse the decision of whether to negotiate or not, including the potential costs and benefits. Examine factors such as your interests, the other side's interests, your alternatives to the commercial negotiation, the shape of a potential deal, the various costs you might incur, and the likelihood that you can successfully follow through on a deal".

Is Everything Really Negotiable?

Tim Cummings of IACCM states" the seminal work on negotiation is the book 'Getting to Yes', written by Fisher and Ury. This book was really designed for a different era, yet it remains at the core of much teaching on negotiation. It was written in an era when many transactions were satisfied at the time of contract signing, or shortly thereafter". Today, however, many agreements are setting the framework for a relatively long-term output or outcome — driving very different parameters for what we might deem 'success'.

James A. Baker states "We have all heard this so many times that we probably don't stop to think about it anymore. It might be worthwhile to take a moment to really consider that statement: "Everything is negotiable." Is that true? Is everything really negotiable?

Carrie Fisher states "Everything is negotiable – whether or not the commercial negotiation is going to be easy is another thing". The UK Brexit negotiations are a case in point.

Commercial Negotiations

In terms of commercial negotiations there are many elements to a contract that may be "negotiable" – all of these have some form of direct or indirect economic effect on the outcome, these can include:

- Price and Costs

- Quality
- Delivery
- Service Levels
- Warranty period
- Buy back period
- Logistics
- Discount and/or rebate structures

Former CPO Mike Inman at a recent CIPS Annual Conference stated, "Stop negotiating over the price with your suppliers and begin negotiating over the costs". He gave one example where negotiating on price would have resulted in a maximum of 5% of savings, whereas re-engineering the way the service was delivered resulted in 30%. This approach, he said, requires procurement professionals to look at the specifications, requirements, demands and design and see where waste occurs.

Negotiating Contract Terms and Conditions
While the above list is easy to recognise, the commercial negotiation of contract terms and conditions may be less so. Express terms and conditions mostly not determined by legislation as our implied terms and therefore can be negotiated. Either party may state that our terms and conditions are non-negotiable, but that is their business decision. In other words – terms and conditions are not set in stone. These negotiables could include:

- Financial safeguards, e.g., bank guarantees, and performance bonds
- Long term product support
- Product guarantee conditions
- Supplier's exclusion clause proposals.
- Insurance requirements e.g., values and whether 'per claim' or "in the aggregate"
- Termination clauses and consequences for both parties
- Price review mechanisms on long term contracts, e.g. indexation
- Use of licenses for computer software and payment, e.g. site licence or user numbers
- Force Majeure – what is included and excluded
- Rights to Intellectual Property in design and copyright.
- Use of sub-contractors and flow down of contract conditions
- Charges for commissioning of IT Software
- Arbitration and dispute resolution rights under contract

- Jurisdiction in the event of dispute
- Mobilisation charges on major projects.
- Liquidated or Unliquidated Damages

IACCM research indicates the following as the most frequently challenged and negotiated contract terms are:

- Limitations of liability
- Price
- Intellectual Property Rights (IPR)
- Indemnities

Fundamental Questions

Before considering the added value of conducting commercial negotiations, we need to address some of the fundamental questions, these include:

- What are we trying to secure?
- When do we need it?
- What is our budget?
- What is really fit for our purpose?
- Who should provide the resource?
- What are the risks/rewards?
- What is the market situation?

Negotiation Outcomes

Herb Cohen, famous American negotiator states, "A successful commercial negotiation occurs when both sides discover an outcome they prefer over the status quo". The map is not the territory, we all see the world in different ways, based upon our life experiences and interests and this will no doubt influence our expectations regarding outcomes.

There are several potential outcomes from any commercial negotiations, these include:

- No deal (Neutral): This is a situation whereby there is no mutually acceptable outcome agreed, both parties feel that they cannot reach agreement. However, both sides retain their mutual respect and trust for each other and therefore future commercial negotiations are possible.
- No deal (Lose-Lose): This is where both sides are faced with disillusionment and frustration. There is a loss of respect and the

relationship is impaired or damaged. Often both sides entered into the commercial negotiation with the intention of reaching a mutually acceptable agreement, but circumstances and or external factors beyond their control intervene to prevent an acceptable outcome. The UK needs to negotiate its exit from the UK. On the one hand, a clear majority voted in the 23 June referendum for Britain to leave the EU but on the other, leave supporters did not vote for a specific version of Brexit – hard or soft. The Hard "exit" outcome with its dire predictions of recession, high unemployment and rapid economic decline will not make the government popular, even with those who voted to leave, whereas "soft" exit outcomes, whereby so much EU legislation and controls will remain in place, may not feel like exit at all. This could result in a lose/lose outcome for the UK negotiators, from a political perspective.

- Deal through domination (Win-Lose): This is where one side due to its market position (sole provider or buyer) and or its bargaining position can impose on the other side an agreement that is not agreement but an unfair imposition. This outcome is not normally sustainable. UK supermarkets are sometimes quoted as seeking win/lose outcomes with farmers. For example cheese has been produced below the cost of production because supermarkets buyers have the power to force the price of milk down. Britain leaving the EU would not make it better. The worst-case scenario is that the subsidies will go and then so would farming. Subsidies are unpopular with the public, but without it last year many farms would have to close with immediate effect.
- Mutual benefit (Win-Win): These are characterised by a process that better integrates the aims and goals of all the involved negotiating parties through creative and collaborative problem solving.

Most and Least Desirable Outcomes

Outcomes can also be expressed in terms of commercial outcomes. These can be in terms of price, delivery, service level and any other negotiable. This approach sets the parameters of the negotiation and often both sides will seek to find the so called "sweet spot" or the Zone of Possible Agreement (ZOPA) which is the middle ground between the two parties.

These parameters can include:

- Most Desirable Outcome (MDO)
- Least Desirable Outcome (LDO)

The Zone of Possible Agreement (ZOPA)

To determine whether there is a positive bargaining zone each party must understand their own LDO. For example, company Alpha wants to charge at least $50,000 for its consulting services, its LDO. The client is interested and negotiates with Alpha. If the client offers Alpha anything in excess of $50,000 that is a positive bargaining zone, if however, the client only wants to pay no more than $45,500 there is a negative bargaining zone. Therefore, a ZOPA exists if there is an overlap between each party's reservation price or LDO. A negative bargaining zone is when there is no overlap. In the situation where there is a negative bargaining zone both parties may walk away.

Best Alternative to Negotiated Agreement (BATNA)

This is the most advantageous alternative course of action that one party can take if commercial negotiations fail. However, the BATNA is not simply a further reduction in the LDO. The BATNA is a viable alternative means of securing the outcome required. It will not be ideal, but it will be fit for purpose.

For example, Delta are negotiating with a local supplier of vehicles for use by the staff. The supplier is being "unreasonable" and is demanding a high price. The objective is to secure transport for staff trips. Therefore, the BATNA could be:

- Set up a framework agreement will local vehicle hire company to provide cars as and when needed
- Encourage staff to make use public transport for shorter trips and claim their expenses
- Re-start selection process re suppliers outside of the area
- Review the vehicle specification

The Symptoms of Ineffective Negotiations

There are many observable symptoms of less than effective commercial negotiations. This list does not identify the root cause of these failings, which will be addressed in the later chapters. These failings can include:

No Agreement

If the parties cannot reach agreement, then the commercial negotiations cannot be deemed to have been a success. Cranfield School of Management state "The UK aspiration to negotiate a free trade agreement with the EU is no more than that, an aspiration."

Creates Disputes
As the commercial negotiations progress more disputes and areas of disagreements arise between the parties as it becomes apparent that their relative positions are poles apart.

Time Consuming
Negotiations sometimes (especially in low value situations) that continue beyond the point at which any added value could have been derived by commercial negotiation has been lost in terms of time and resource devoted to the process.

Tension and stress
Difficult commercial negotiation situations can create tensions between the parties which can in turn can stress those involved and may make staff reluctant to become involved or just simply accept what is offered by the other side.

Lose/Lose Outcomes
In some instances, neither side can derive any benefit from the process, and both end up in a less than optimal situation. A good example, is the potential outcome form the UK exit commercial negotiations. On the one hand, a clear majority voted in the 23 June referendum for Britain to leave the EU but on the other, leave supporters did not vote for a specific version of Brexit – hard or soft.

The Hard "exit" outcome with its dire predictions of recession, high unemployment and rapid economic decline will not make the government popular, even with those who voted to leave. Whereas "soft" exit outcomes, whereby so much EU legislation and controls will remain in place, may not feel like exit at all. Therefore, the UK negotiators (from a political point of view) are in a potential no win or lose/lose situation.

Dead ends
This is characterised by both sides negotiating into a cul de sac or dead end. Both sides will not move positions or demonstrate flexibility and the commercial negotiation turns into a head banging session will dialogue like "Yes you will and no I will not" and no side makes progress toward a settlement.

Frustration
The outcome of dead ends and no agreement is obviously frustration, which leads to tension and stress amongst the negotiators and this in turn can affect the efficiency of the process.

Deception

When either side starts to lose their integrity by resorting to lies and deceptions, then this is clear evidence that the commercial negotiations are not proceeding to plan. There is real risk of achieving a unsustainable outcome. When these "misrepresentations" are used to induce either side to agree to a settlement, that later turns out not be true, a legal claim can ensue.

A good case is that of Esso v Mardon. Esso's experienced representative told Mardon that Esso estimated that the throughput of petrol at the station would reach 200,000 gallons in the third year of operation and so persuaded Mardon to enter into a tenancy agreement for three years. However, the site was not good enough to achieve that throughput. Mardon lost money and was unable to pay for petrol supplied. Esso claimed possession of the site and money due. Mardon claimed and won damages in respect of the representation made by Esso during the commercial negotiations.

The Added Value of Effective Commercial Negotiations

A good example of the added value of effective commercial relationships is in the Advertising Agency market. In the past clients had only one choice when it came to advertising, they went to a large established Agency.

These Agencies had three talents – they had clever ideas, they could turn those into clever images, and they could wave a sparkly wand and make them appear all over the place. Clients now want to see just how their money is being spent – how those ideas were turned into press adverts and mail-shots, and who actually delivered them and procurement was empowered to negotiate. Lloyds Banking Group made use of effective commercial negotiations with suppliers and contractors to generate significant savings.

Here is an example of where commercial negotiation could have saved millions. NHS officials have been accused of failing to adequately check price hikes for medicines, resulting in additional costs of £125m. An investigation found the UK company AMCO bought up licences for old drugs and raised prices by up to 600%.

The Phases of Negotiating

The process of commercial negotiations tends to include the following phases:

- Planning
- Preparation
- Opening
- Negotiating including conditioning, compromising, bargaining, influencing, persuading

- Agreement
- Confirming

Each of these phases will be explored in more detail in later chapters.

Basis of Negotiating Power

The negotiation power of either side in a commercial negotiation is a function of the relative bargaining positions of either side. Negotiating power exists to the extent that both parties accept it as being powerful. IACCM states that commercial negotiation power is:

- Enhanced by information
- Enhanced by the ability to endure uncertainty (potential risk) and by commitment
- Enhanced by a good negotiating relationship
- Enhanced by a sound BATNA

Julia Hanna of the HBR states "Wal-Mart, the world's largest retailer, with its single-minded focus on "EDLP" (everyday low prices) and the power to make or break suppliers, a partnership with Wal-Mart is either the Holy Grail or the kiss of death, depending on one's perspective".

Arbitration and Mediation

In almost all cases disputes between the contractor and the client can be negotiated to a mutually acceptable conclusion. However, in some cases this is not possible and both sides will then agree to seek mediation and or arbitration.

Definitions

Arbitration is a voluntary judicial process to ascertain, declare and enforce the respective rights and obligations of the parties to a contract. Client's contracts generally include a clause which provides for resolution through arbitration. The arbitration tribunal is normally composed of three arbitrators two appointed by the parties and an Umpire agreed upon by the said two arbitrators.

Mediation (sometimes referred to as Alternative Dispute Resolution) is used when people want to resolve a dispute but avoid the Courts. The UK government is encouraging the use of ADR to relieve the pressure on the courts. The UK government wants to encourage the development of ADR. It states that "Better ADR and easier access to it should also be good for all businesses committed to giving their customers the best possible service". (Alternative Dispute Regulations 2015)

Regulations

There are two sets of regulations that have been laid in Parliament to implement the European Directive on alternative dispute resolution (ADR) in the UK.

- The Alternative Dispute Resolution for Consumer Disputes (Competent Authorities and Information) Regulations 2015
- The Alternative Dispute Resolution for Consumer Disputes (Amendment) Regulations 2015.

These regulations are designed to:

- Place an information requirement on businesses selling to consumers
- Establish competent authorities to certify ADR schemes
- Set the standards that ADR scheme applicants must meet in order to achieve certification

These regulations do not make participation in ADR schemes mandatory for companies. However, the regulations do require almost all businesses which sell directly to consumers to point the consumer to a certified ADR scheme – when they cannot resolve a dispute in-house – and declare whether they intend to use that scheme.

The regulations also require that ADR providers wishing to gain certification must meet certain standards regarding independence, impartiality, and quality of expertise.

Mediation Process

When all parties agree to meditation, the mediator will facilitate the parties to come to the meeting and bring together both parties and their advisers and replace confrontation with principled and win/win style negotiation.

ADR is recognised as the most confidential and cost-effective way of settling a dispute. What can cause disputes?

- The interpretation of a contract term
- Misunderstanding about requirements/Schedule of Works (SOW)
- Late delivery, late payment, poor quality and service
- The desire of one party to change or vary contract terms

A three-year dispute between Starbucks and Kraft Foods over distribution of Starbucks packaged coffee in grocery stores was finally resolved by arbitration ruling that Starbucks had breached its agreement with Kraft. The coffeemaker was ordered to pay the food giant $2.75 billion.

Chapter Summary

In this chapter we have considered:

- What is meant by commercial negotiations?
- When is it not advisable to enter commercial negotiations?
- We defined the different types of outcomes, including BATNA, MDO and LDO
- Identified the symptoms of poorly managed negotiations
- The role of Arbitration and Mediation in settling disputes
- The advantages of effective commercial negotiations and the phases in the process
- What is negotiable in commercial contracts, including terms and conditions

---

Case Study

Ms Rasha is the head of technical research at Fosters, a UK based company in the oil and gas sector. She needs to commission Grantham Research consultants to undertake a large research project into the attitudes of people to the concept Health and Safety in the field. The aim is gain an insight into why some ethnic groups are reluctant to follow HSE rules. Rashad has a meeting with Peter Grantham, the head of Grantham Research and they discuss the project in only general terms. She then sends Grantham an email dated 5th which states:

"Hi Peter, as per our conversation last week, please go ahead with the research. I need this done by the end of the month as I am speaking at the National HSE Conference. As we discussed I need you to find out why some people do not want to be safe! I also accept your estimated cost of £350,000 for this work".

A few weeks later the Peter sends the report to Rashad, but she finds that he has not collected or analysed the data she requires. Fundamentally, it does not differentiate between the various ethnic groups and therefore is of little value, plus the invoice submitted by Peter is for £600,000. She calls Peter to discuss the issue. He states that he has delivered as per the email sent on the 5th and does not recall any reference to ethnic groups. The figure of £35,000 was only an estimate and if Rasha required a firm price she should have asked. She is very angry at this and states that "Peter knew

---

exactly what my requirements were…" Rashad decides to call Peter to a meeting to negotiate a resolution.

Task
    1. Does Rashad have a case?
    2. What should be her MDO, LDO and BATNA?
    3. How could this dispute have been avoided?

CHAPTER 2 | BUILDING THE NEGOTIATION TEAM

Definitions

The *Business Dictionary* defines a team as "A group of people with a full set of complementary skills required to complete a task, job, or project. Team members operate with a high degree of interdependence, share authority and responsibility for self-management, are accountable for the collective performance, and work toward a common goal and shared rewards.

A team becomes more than just a collection of people when a strong sense of mutual commitment creates synergy, thus generating performance greater than the sum of the performance of its individual members".

In the context of forming a team to negotiate a large strategic contract, it would be difficult to find a better statement of what is required.

Showing empathy with the challenge's suppliers face in a negotiation can help relationships go further.

Beth Loudon, head of procurement development and sourcing at NHS Shared Business Services (SBS), said she had worked in both business development and purchasing at the organisation and the two functions faced many of the same internal blockers and that showing empathy with the challenge's suppliers face in a negotiation can help relationships go further.

Belbin Study

The Belbin Team Role Inventory was devised in the 1970s by Meredith Belbin to measure preference for nine Team Roles. He had identified eight of those whilst studying numerous teams at Henley Management College in the UK.

Belbin defines a Team Role as "a tendency to behave, contribute and interrelate with others in a particular way."

Belbin identified nine different behaviours that individuals display in the work place. There are nine Belbin Team Roles, these descriptions are taken from the Belbin official website.

Resource Investigator

They use their inquisitive nature to find ideas to bring back to the team.

- Strengths: Outgoing, enthusiastic, explores opportunities and develops contacts

- Allowable weaknesses: Might be over-optimistic, and can lose interest once the initial enthusiasm has passed
- However, they might forget to follow up on a lead

Their role in the commercial negotiations process could include networking with stakeholders, giving feedback on negotiation progress and the impact upon relationships, could be one of the face-to-face negotiators.

Team worker
Helps the team to gel, using their versatility to identify the work required and complete it on behalf of the team.

- Strengths: Co-operative, perceptive, and diplomatic, listens and averts friction
- Allowable weaknesses: Can be indecisive in crunch situations and tends to avoid confrontation
- However, they might be hesitant to make unpopular decisions

Their role in the commercial negotiations process could include developing the commodity guide, desk research regarding relative bargaining positions, encouragement of fellow team members to strive for optimum outcomes.

The "Co-ordinator"
Needed to focus on the team's objectives, draw out team members and delegate work appropriately.

- Strengths: Mature, confident, identifies talent, clarifies goals.
- Allowable weaknesses: Can be perceived as manipulative and might offload their own share of the work
- They might over-delegate, leaving themselves little work

Their role in the commercial negotiations process could include encouraging focus on obtaining desired optimum and sustainable outcomes, delegation of roles such as planning and preparation tasks.

The "Plant"
Tend to be highly creative and good at solving problems in unconventional ways.

- Strengths: Creative, imaginative, free-thinking, generates ideas and solves difficult problems

- Allowable weaknesses: Might ignore incidentals, and may be too preoccupied to communicate effectively
- However, they can be absent minded or forgetful

Their role in the commercial negotiations process could include developing negotiation strategies and innovative solutions to problems to achieve sustainable and mutually acceptable outcomes, could be involved in the face-to-face negotiations.

The "Monitor Evaluator"
Provides a logical eye, making impartial judgements where required and weighs up the team's options in a dispassionate way.

- Strengths: Sober, strategic, and discerning, sees all options and judges accurately
- Allowable weaknesses: Sometimes lacks the drive and ability to inspire others and can be overly critical
- However, they can be slow to come to a decision

Their role in the negotiations process could include critical evaluation of offers made or received during the negotiations, will only be persuaded by logical and sustainable arguments, not easily swayed by marketing ploys.

The "Specialist"
They bring in-depth knowledge of a key area to the team.

- Strengths: Single-minded, self-starting and dedicated, they provide specialist knowledge and skills
- Allowable weaknesses: Tends to contribute on a narrow front and can dwell on the technicalities
- However, they may overload you with information

Their role in the negotiations process could include background information about the product or service, evaluating alternative technical solutions suggested by the contractor, some involvement in the face-to-face negotiations, at appropriate stages of the discussions.

The "Shaper"
They provide the necessary drive to ensure that the team keeps moving and does

not lose focus or momentum.

- Strengths: Challenging, dynamic, thrives on pressure, has the drive and courage to overcome obstacles
- Allowable weaknesses: Can be prone to provocation, and may sometimes offend people's feelings
- However, they could risk becoming aggressive and bad-humoured in their attempts to get things done.

Their role in the negotiations process could include setting up the negotiations, selecting the team, determining the outcomes and develops the strategy, will take responsibility for the face-to-face negotiations success or failure.

The "Implementer"
They are needed to plan a workable strategy and carry it out as efficiently as possible.

- Strengths: Practical, reliable, efficient, turns ideas into actions and organises work that needs to be done
- Allowable weaknesses: Can be a bit inflexible and slow to respond to new possibilities
- However, they might be slow to relinquish their plans in favour of positive changes

Their role in the commercial negotiations process could include, once agreement has been reached, they will take responsibility for writing up of agreements and execution of contracts and the mobilisation process.

The "Completer Finisher"
Most effectively used at the end of tasks to polish and scrutinise the work for errors, subjecting it to the highest standards of quality control.

- Strengths: Painstaking, conscientious, anxious. Searches out errors. Polishes and perfects
- Allowable weaknesses: Can be inclined to worry unduly, and reluctant to delegate
- Don't be surprised to find that: They could be accused of taking their perfectionism to extremes

Their role in the negotiations process could include checking draft agreements, writing up of the negotiation narrative, checking facts and figures.

A Belbin Individual Report

A Belbin Individual Report identifies which combination of the nine Belbin Team Roles someone prefers. They are easy to generate and cost around £50. Respondents complete an online questionnaire, and within minutes receive an email with their Belbin Individual Report. This could be a very useful resource when building a negotiation team.

In the article *Unlocking a Project Team's High-Performance Potential Using Cognitive Readiness* (Archibald, R. & Di Filippo, I. (2013). *Unlocking a Project Team's High-Performance Potential Vol. II*, Issue XI. www.pmworldjournal.net) they define a High-Performance Team:

"As a group of people with specific roles and complementary talents and skills, aligned with and committed to a common purpose, who consistently show high levels of collaboration and innovation, and who produce superior results. The high-performance team is regarded as tight-knit and focused on their goals. Team members are so devoted to their purpose that they will do all that is humanly possible to surmount any barrier to achieve the team's goals."

They go on to make the point that "There is a sense of clear focus and intense energy within a high-performance team. Collectively, the team has its own consciousness, indicating shared norms and values within the team. The team feels a strong sense of accountability for achieving their goals. Team members display high levels of mutual trust towards each other."

Importance of an Effective Team

To be able manage effective commercial negotiations, the team needs to be able to:
- Plan and fully prepare for the commercial negotiation
- Apply a range of commercial negotiation strategies and tactics to achieve set and desired outcomes
- Differentiate and utilize a range of persuasion and influencing tools and techniques
- Appreciate that different approaches are required when negotiating in different contexts for example competitive v oligopolistic market
- Understand how to analyse its commercial negotiation performance and to constantly learn and develop

It is important that the team members clearly understand their role and responsibilities and often this type of table is used.

Team Member	Role/Responsibility
Sally	Lead Negotiator
Ben and Mary	Negotiators
Ali	Technical Support
Geoff and Lesley	Corporate
Pam and Sam	Finance/Commercial Analyst

Roles and Responsibilities of the Team Members

- The Lead Negotiator is responsible for ensuring the objectives of the negotiation are met and the rules for negotiation (as detailed in the plan) are followed.
- One Negotiation Team member must minute all negotiated outcomes and provide minutes to all members of both parties for agreement.
- All Negotiation Team members are to be present at all negotiations, unless they have been given an 'as required' status.
- The Lead Negotiator may approve the attendance of additional advisors or subject matter experts if required
- The Lead Negotiator will obtain appropriate authority prior to negotiations to allow commitment to appropriate negotiated outcomes as they occur
- Negotiation Team Sign Off

It is important that all documents, reports and information discussed within the negotiation must be treated by the team as commercial-in-confidence. Information and documentation must always be kept secure and not be divulged or given to any persons not directly involved in the negotiation process.

The EU announced a 30-strong squad of officials who will help thrash out the terms of Brexit with Theresa May when she triggered Article 50. However, none of them have any experience of dealing with Britain, raising the prospect that a lack of understanding and expertise on both sides of the Channel could hamper smooth talks, which is what has occurred.

Effective Negotiators

Negotiators need to be able to plan, prepare and undertake effective commercial negotiations, demonstrating high levels of personal effectiveness, and achieving best value across the supply chain. We have simplified this down to the Five Ps:

- Plan
- Prepare by understanding all the relevant facts, figures, market conditions and relative bargaining positions of both sides
- Participate in professional and appropriate manner, making use of a "principled" approach to negotiations
- Perform and secure the objectives within the ZOPA
- Post evaluation of their performance and to learn the lessons to improve

The following chapters will cover these basic requirements and many other important aspects of commercial negotiation

Experience

Norway's prime minister has stated that Britain's four-decade membership of the EU has left it lacking experience in international commercial negotiations, which will hamper it in trade talks and may lead to "a very hard Brexit".

IACCM states "The strategic contracts professional must constantly review shifts in technology, business practice and legislation to ensure that their approach to contracting is competitive, low cost and facilitates the ease of doing business".

Attributes of Effective Negotiators

A negotiator can be successful in one scenario, but less effective in another. What makes an effective negotiator? Before we can address this, we need to define what we mean by "effective".

An effective negotiator in a traditional win-or-lose negotiation situation for high stakes might not have the same success when dealing with a long-term supplier with whom he or she has a valued relationship. In negotiation, it is often the context that determines how we measure the effectiveness of the individuals involved.

The characteristics of an Effective Negotiator

These can be defined as distinguishing features or qualities and can include:

- Competency: what the person can do. "She is able to analyse the supply market."
- Knowledge: what the person knows. "He understands the legal implications of exclusion clauses."
- Skill: proficiency, facility or dexterity that is acquired or developed through training experience or practice. "She can communicate very clearly."

- Personality traits: what the person is like. "He is an extrovert – an outgoing and lively negotiator."

There are some characteristics that are useful regardless of the context: being an effective communicator, for example. But a trait such as ruthlessness could be critical in a classic win-or-lose situation. Negotiation competencies, including cognitive ability, emotional intelligence, and a sense of perspective, are often cited as the key classifications. Added to this is the negotiator's experience and learning's overtime. This reflects that the build-up of experience is not just about the number of negotiation sessions the negotiator has undertaken.

We could say the characteristic of effective negotiators is that they achieve their objectives. In a episode of the BBC's *The Bottom Line*, presenter Evan Davis asked his guests what makes an effective negotiator. They cited being firm and fair, having a "bottom line" taking account of the relationship and the context. Interestingly, two out of three of these "deal-makers" had never had any formal negotiation training. Maybe these are the exception that makes the rule.

It is well known that people can be knowledgeable but not necessarily competent. But it is quite difficult to be a competent negotiator without a sound knowledge base and training.

Writers such as Howard Raiffa and Tracy Harwood have listed many of the characteristics of an effective negotiator, such as verbal expression, integrity, planning skills and judgment. Neil Rackham identifies the characteristics in relation to the three main phases of the negotiation process – pre-negotiation, meeting, and post-negotiation. He cites the ability to evaluate more outcome options for the issues to be discussed as a key characteristic at the pre-negotiation stage.

Personality Types and Profiles
Obviously, the personality type of team members will also be an influence in the style of negotiations and their relative roles and responsibilities of team members. The profiles below are based upon personality and emotional stability. We often find that the extrovert/stable makes an effective negotiator and will normally adopt a win/win approach whereas introvert/unstable is often not comfortable with the face-to-face aspects of negotiation.

Extrovert/unstable is more likely to adopt a more traditional win/lose completive style of commercial negotiation. Introvert/stable tend to be likened to Belbin's evaluator and will work in the back ground developing strategy and evaluating options. This matrix is also useful to gain an insight into the typical behaviours and reactions of those on the other side of the table, providing one has knowledge of their personality and stability in advance or gained from previous negotiations.

Chapter Summary
In this chapter we have considered:

- The building an effective negotiating team
- The role of Belbin Types in contract and commercial negotiations
- The profile and characteristics of an effective negotiator
- Roles and responsibilities of team members in contract and commercial negotiations

Case Study
Innovative Medical ltd are a niche medical equipment company involved in the development of innovative and specialist medical equipment. The company relies on their suppliers and contractors to come to them with their ideas and innovations to enable them to develop these into innovatitive medical solutions and technologies. Although the relationship between Innovative medical and its suppliers is very close and collaborative, it's still a "commercial "relationship.

Therefore, the company must negotiate with its suppliers to secure value for money, this is made more difficult because some of these suppliers would be defined as bottleneck and or sole source. Ms Ann Parker, who is the head of contracts at Innovative Medical must decide who to send to the USA to negotiate with one of these key suppliers for the supply critical software for which their own the IPR. The USA negotiators and quite tough and know how to leverage their bargaining strengths

Tim and Sally are both members of the negotiating Innovative Medical team and are keen to undertake this assignment. Tim is a very outgoing type and feels he is good with people. Tim has a reputation for being a tough negotiator and does not flinch from using some of the many tactics and ploys often associated with traditional win/lose negotiations. Tim is very results focused and can get quite angry if he feels he is being frustrated by the other side or they are being unreasonable in his view.

Sally has a reputation for achieving her negotiation objectives and will often develop a BATNA. Sally is good with people and has good emotional intelligence and can read people quite well. She is very focused and does not give into pressure. She always keepers her temper and is dogged in her approach to secure a win/win agreement.

Task

Taking the role of Ann Parker, who would you send to the USA and why?

CHAPTER 3 | PREPARATION AND PLANNING FOR CONTRACT AND COMMERCIAL NEGOTIATIONS

Definitions

Meina Liu & Sabine Chai in their book *Planning and Preparation for Effective Negotiation* (Liu, Meina & Chai, Sabine. (2011). Planning and Preparing for Effective Negotiation. 10.1142/9789814343176_0002.) state that "The first, and often the most important step toward successful negotiation is planning and preparation".

About 80% of negotiators' efforts should go toward the preparation stage, but that is not always the case and suboptimal and unstainable outcomes are often the result.

They go on to state "However, planning and preparation go beyond what negotiators should do before negotiation. Negotiation is a dynamic communication process where new information, concerns, emotions, and goals may arise, negotiators should also be prepared for dealing with contingencies as well as factors that may interfere with goal pursuit".

Purpose and Objectives of Negotiation

In terms of commodities we do not spend much time thinking about value creation or collaboration. We negotiate on price against standard quality and technical standards. However, in the case of strategic and bottleneck categories then the purpose of negotiation is about maximizing value creation for both sides. IACCM states that "Most negotiations result in value opportunities being missed and left untapped by either party".

Research by Keld Jensen, Chairman of the Centre for Negotiation at Copenhagen Business School, shows that in a typical negotiation, the supplier achieves a 39% share of the total value available from the deal, while the purchaser achieves 19% of the total value available from the deal. The supplier and contract manager spend time and effort trying to take a piece of the other's share, moving value from one of those two segments to the other.

The strategic picture that is missed is that both sides fail to recognize and capitalize upon the opportunity to gain part of the other 42% of the value available from the deal, which represents unutilized added value.

Preparing for Negotiations

It is often said that preparation is the most important part of the negotiation process and often cases where negotiations have failed or have led to sub optimal outcomes for one side can be traced back to lack of preparation on the part of one or indeed both sides. The UK's negotiation with the EU is case in point.

Fundamental Questions

Obviously, there are some fundamental facts, figures and context that need to be researched and established prior to developing our negotiation objectives, SWOT and strategies. These will include:

- Our aims and objectives
- Stakeholder requirements
- Market conditions
- Our leverage with suppliers
- Contract classification – strategic, leverage or bottleneck
- Our relationship

However, to be fully prepared there may be a need to undertake a more granular investigation of those broad headings.

HBS Negotiation Preparation Checklist

Katie Shonk, who is the editor of Negotiation Briefings at the Harvard Law School and a research associate for Harvard Business School USA, has developed a very comprehensive and granular Negotiation Preparation Checklist, in which she states that "Our negotiation preparation checklist will position you to prepare as thoroughly as necessary to create value and claim value in your next important business negotiation". These questions include the following:

1. What do I want from this negotiation? List short-term and long-term goals and dreams related to the negotiation.
2. What are my strengths—values, skills, and assets—in this negotiation?
3. What are my weaknesses and vulnerabilities in this negotiation?
4. Why is the other party negotiating with me? What do I have that they need?
5. What lessons can I apply from past negotiations to improve my performance?
6. Where and when should the negotiation take place?

7. How long should talks last? What deadlines are we facing?
8. What are my interests in the upcoming negotiation? How do they rank in importance?
9. What is my best alternative to a negotiated agreement, or BATNA? That is, what option would I turn to if I'm not satisfied with the deal we negotiate or if we reach an impasse? How can I strengthen my BATNA?
10. What is my reservation point—my indifference point between a deal and no deal?
11. What is my aspiration point in the negotiation—the ambitious, but not outrageous, goal that I'd like to reach?
12. What are the other side's interests? How important might each issue be to them?
13. What do I think their reservation point and BATNA may be? How can I find out more?
14. What does their BATNA mean in terms of their willingness to do a deal with me? Who has more power to walk away?
15. Is there a zone of possible agreement (ZOPA) between my reservation point and the other side's? If there clearly is no room for bargaining, then there's no reason to negotiate—but don't give up until you're sure. You may be able to add more issues to the discussion.
16. What is my relationship history with the other party? How might our past relationship affect current talks?
17. Are there cultural differences that we should prepare for?
18. To what degree will we be negotiating electronically? Are we prepared for the pros and cons of negotiating via email, teleconference, etc.?
19. In what order should I approach various parties on the other side?
20. What is the hierarchy within the other side's team? What are the patterns of influence and potential tensions? How might these internal dynamics affect talks?
21. What potential ethical pitfalls should we keep in mind during the negotiation?
22. Who are my competitors for this deal? How do our relative advantages and disadvantages compare?
23. What objective benchmarks, criteria, and precedents will support my preferred position?
24. Who should be on my negotiating team? Who should be our spokesperson? What specific responsibilities should each team member have?
25. Do we need to involve any third parties (agents, lawyers, mediators, interpreters)?

26. What authority do I have (or does our team have) to make firm commitments?
27. Am I ready to engage in interest-based bargaining? Be prepared to try to create value by trading on differences in resources, preferences, forecasts, risk tolerance, and deadlines.
28. If we disagree about how the future plays out, can we explore a contingency contract—that is, stipulate what will happen if each side's prediction comes true?
29. What parties not yet involved in the negotiation might also value an agreement?
30. Have I practiced communicating my message to the other side? How are they likely to respond?
31. Does the agenda make room for simultaneous discussion of multiple issues?
32. Is an agreement likely to create net value for society? How can we reduce potential harm to outside parties?

Stakeholder Engagement

One of the keys to successful commercial negotiations is gaining the support and requirements from the organisation's key stakeholders. There is a need to create a "shared vision" regarding the desired outcomes, expectations, risks and constraints, prior to developing the strategy or undertaking the negotiations. The failure of the UK Prime Minster to gain the support of some of her MP's prior or even during her negotiations with the EU is good example of how damaging this can be.

Jennette Nyden's checklist

Nyden, co-author of *Getting to We* (Nyden, J., Vitasek, K., Frydlinger, D. (2013). *Getting to We: Negotiating Agreements for Highly Collaborative Relationships.* Palgrave MacMillan) has developed a checklist to assist in the process of managing and engaging with stakeholders, this includes:

- What stakeholders need to help develop the shared vision?
- Who will facilitate the process internal or external?
- Will an internal facilitator need to participate process as a stakeholder?
- How much time can each party dedicate to this process
- What preparatory work should each stakeholder?

The head of the negotiation team needs to take responsibility for stakeholder engagement and the use of a facilitated focus group event is often the most effective and time efficient method.

Understanding the Supply Market

Gaining an understanding of current market conditions, available resources, maturity, levels of competence and competition are an essential of the preparation process. Market Testing is an exercise to gain an insight into the feasibility, practicality and deliverability of a project or service. The client invites all providers to participate in soft market testing exercise to refine the final specification and develop a negotiation position.

- Prevents time-wasting
- Gather market intelligence
- Gain insights into options and
- Clear and robust specifications and scopes of work

Supply Market Analysis – Porter's Five Forces

Porter's model (see fig 1) is a very well-established tool for undertaking an analysis of the market forces that affect competition. It is framed around three forces from 'horizontal' competition, the threat of substitute products or services, the threat of established rivals, and the threat of new entrants. The two others from 'vertical' competition the bargaining power of suppliers and the bargaining power of customers. Negotiators can utilize market intelligence when developing their objective, scope development, negotiation strategy, cost estimate, trends, negotiations and market analysis.

Figure 1: Porter's Five Forces

Case History

The UK Domiciliary Care Market

We recently worked with a local Authority (LA) in the UK to help their Domiciliary Care team better understand the local market place and the factors that affect the provision of these services in terms of availability and cost. The assignment was framed around Porter's 5 Forces of Competition. Local Authorities spends millions on the provision of these services. These provision of these services are a UK statutory function and therefore must be provided by LA. The challenge of providing these services within the budgets set is one facing almost all Local Authorities across the UK. There are also doubts that the commercial model used to pay providers for these services is sustainable. Only recently a major UK home care provider, who provides support to 13,000 older and disabled people, sought to transfer or sell all its contracts to other providers. Allied Healthcare was warned by the care regulator about its financial sustainability.

The team first researched the power of the suppliers, which was significant given that current demand often outstrips supply and providers can ask for more as ceiling rates allow for negotiation. The impact of Brexit on the supplier's staff resourcing could have a significant impact upon just how much of this service they will be able to provide at the current rate of compensation. There is a reluctance on the party of the providers to embrace new technology and thus they can control the flow of information about what services they can supply. It is also significant that the two largest local providers still only account for 20% of the total hours provide and most other suppliers account for 5% or less each.

Next the team reviewed the issues of risk of new entrants, that might weaken the bargaining position of these local powerful providers. The Domiciliary Care sector is relatively easy to enter. However, it is highly regulated, and lack of labour does restrict new entrants to some degree. There is also the attraction of the more lucrative private sector thus limiting new entrants to the purely publicly funded market. The issue of low profit margins and return on capital employed is also a significant inhibitor.

The issue of buyer power was the next factor to be examined. LAs are the main buyer of these services across most boroughs. LA's reputation as an efficient and effective council has helped their providers secure more contracts by that positive association with the LA "brand".

As the major customer of these servicers, LA has significant power in shaping the home care delivery model and the local market. However, there are other buyers on the scene, for example neighbouring LAs or individuals who are self-funding. These tend to weaken the power of the buyer. LA can set a realistic pricing framework and can stop using providers if the level of quality falls below the required standard. However, LA has very high demand and the local market has yet to meet that level of demand, so it is very much a sellers' market.

The supply of substitute services is also a key factor in Porter's Model and this can either strengthen or weaken both the buyers' and suppliers' bargaining position. The main substitute for council provision of these services is the Direct Payments option and the employment of personal assistants. In this option, the individual claims an allowance from the council and is the responsible for organising their own care. This can be in the form of employing relatives to provide these services.

The last factor in the model is that of the inherent rivalry between the providers and the extent to which they are prepared to compete aggressively for market share. Overall the team found relatively low levels of rivalry between the local providers, this is not surprising given the imbalance between supply and demand. Geographical dominance by some providers also limits the sense of rivalry and the providers have no real sense of brand or brand differentiation which is key to developing a more robust and competitive market place.

This research and subsequent analysis indicated that the suppliers of these services often perceive LA (and many other Local Authorities) as being unattractive clients and coupled with the low rates leads to them being categorised as a "nuisance" client. This has led to a realisation that the council needs to change that negative perception to that of core client, based upon an increase in the volume of work via leverage with one two larger suppliers. The use of new technology to improve the efficiency of the service provided could help to improve the profit margins of providers. This could include all local providers who are on a database which indicates their available resource and the application of route planning to avoid traffic issues.

The LA also felt that there is a real opportunity for a large player to come and dominate the local market and thus gain the economies of scale and the improvements via the use of new technology. Encouraging people to opt for the Direct Payment option could also help to create more competition, this could be facilitated by reaching out to service users to explain how this option works and provide support in the form of guides and templates to assist users in setting up these support services and the administrative and financial systems required.

The outcome from the market analysis feeds into and influences the SWOT analysis exercise.

Understanding the Types of Competition

The table below highlights some of the characteristics of the various types of competition that Porter's analysis will indicate. The commercial negotiator needs to appreciate these different market situations and prepare accordingly for example in the case of imperfect completion, the buyer can expect the supplier to be flexible and responsive to challenges about price, he or she cannot expect that with a true monopoly.

Perfect Competition	Imperfect competition	Oligopoly	Monopoly
Many small suppliers	Many slightly larger suppliers	A few large suppliers	One supplier only
Homogeneous	Products similar and substitutes for one another	Normally, differentiated goods variable substitution between products	One type of product only
One market price	Price competition	No price competition, due to avoidance of price wars.	Price set by one firm ('price maker')
Perfect information	Imperfect information	Imperfect information	Imperfect information
No barriers to entry in the long run	No barriers to entry in the long run	Barriers to entry	Barriers to entry

SWOT Analysis and Relative Bargaining Positions

SWOT Analysis (which many accredit to Albert S. Humphrey) is a very useful technique for understanding Strengths and Weaknesses, and for identifying both the Opportunities and the Threats in the context of preparing for commercial negotiations (see figure 2). It obviously very important to undertake this analysis prior to entering negotiations and developing strategies. Understanding one's own SWOT and that of the supplier is critical to achieving a sustainable outcome.

Strengths	Weaknesses
Opportunities	**Threats**

Figure 2: SWOT

What makes SWOT particularly powerful tool in the context of commercial negotiations is that it can uncover opportunities that can be exploited. By understanding the weaknesses of negotiation position, we can take steps to shield or hid those weakness and to eliminate or mitigate the threats.

Undertaking SWOT Analysis

The pre-negotiation SWOT exercise can be a simple getting key stakeholders together to "brain storm" ideas (or as we now call it "thoughts shower") Or in a more sophisticated way utilizing the focus group approach, facilitated by the head of the negotiating team.

Strengths and weaknesses are often internal to the organization, while opportunities and threats generally relate to external factors.

Strengths

Typical strengths in the context of commercial negotiations could include:

- Our leverage – clients spend to the supplier's turnover
- Buyers' market
- Our track record in terms of payment
- The power of our brand and the value to suppliers by association
- Skilled Team of in-house negotiator's
- Robust BATNA

We also need to consider our strengths from both an internal perspective, and from the perspective of our suppliers and the marketplace.

Weaknesses

Typical weakness in the context of commercial negotiation could include:

- Lack of leverage
- Sellers' market
- Poor track record in terms of payment
- Negative brand image and the damage by association
- Lack of skilled Team of in-house negotiator's
- Weak or non-exist BATNA

Again, we need to consider this from an internal and external perspective, and from the perspective of the suppliers.

Opportunities

Typical opportunities in the context of commercial negotiation could include:

- Develop a more strategic relationship
- Consolidate spend to improve leverage
- Form long-term agreements to secure the resource
- Exploit buyers' market situation
- Develop reciprocal arrangements
- Increase the value gained for both sides
- Win/win outcomes

Threats

Typical threats in the context of commercial negotiation could include:

- Contractor walks out
- Contractor exploits sellers' market
- Outbid by other customers
- Win/lose outcomes

Conducting the SWOT Analysis

When conducting the analysis to ensure that it is accurate and effective, we need the following:

- Precise and verifiable statements
- Concise lists of factors and prioritized and focusing on the most significant factors.
- Options generated are carried through to later stages in the negotiation strategy formation process.
- Used it in conjunction with other strategy tools such as product life cycle Competence Analysis and PEST analysis to gain a comprehensive insight of the relative bargaining positions of both sides' situation

Developing the BATNA

This stands for the Best Alternative to a Negotiated Agreement (BATNA) This means the most advantageous alternative course of action that one party can take if the commercial negotiations fail. However, the BATNA is not simply a further reduction in the least desirable outcome (LDO).

The BATNA is a viable alternative means of securing the outcome required. It may not be ideal, but it will be fit for purpose. The BATNA needs to be established prior to the commencement of commercial negotiations and will need stakeholder approval.

Chapter Summary

In this chapter we have considered:

- The preparation and planning process
- Setting objectives in the context of contract and commercial negotiations
- The opportunities for terms and conditions audit
- Category classification and its impact upon the negotiating process
- Establishing the BATNA and analysing the SWOT and relative bargaining positions
- Analysing the Political, Economic, Social, Technical forces that affect negotiations
- The use of Porter's Five Forces of Competition model
- Cost analysis, concessions and compromise, tradeable and red lines

Case Study

Bratt Pumps

One of the key items bought in by Bratt Pumps Ltd is a small standard motor used in the production of the majority of Bratts' electric pumps. For several years, these motors have been supplied by Brooms Electric, a local distributor of many electrical items to a wide range of engineering companies. This supplier has always been very reliable, with very few delivery or quality problems. However, in recent months Michael, the Commercial Manager at Bratts has become increasingly concerned at the steadily rising price of these motors and, as they are purchased in quite large quantities, Michael is worried about the effects on his total costs.

Brooms revise their price list every six months and, although they give a trade discount of 20% to Bratt, Michael believes that he could obtain these motors more cheaply elsewhere. He is reluctant to change suppliers because of the good relationship which has been built up and because he doubts whether any other supplier would give the same excellent service that Brooms give.

Nevertheless, something must be done. A look at the way in which prices have moved over recent years shows that the list has increased as follows:

Year 1
Jan: £1250
July: £1270

Year 2
Jan: £1300
July: £1330

Year 3
Jan: £1410
July: £1510

During this period, motors have been purchased at a total cost of several million pounds. Michael feels that this level of business merits a larger discount than the one he currently is given. He found out a few weeks ago at a Chamber of Commerce dinner that even the smallest customers are given a 15% discount off list prices.

The trade services journal which Bratt subscribe to is a publication covering prices and costs incurred in the industry. This shows that during the period above, the average rise in motor prices was much lower than that of Brooms. The relevant figures (which cover all electric motors) not just small ones, were:

Year 1
Jan: £114
July: £1160

Year 2
Jan: £119
July: £1230

Year 3
Jan: £125
July: £1280

Taking the role of Bratt, explain how you would prepare for the forthcoming negotiation.

CHAPTER 4 | THE OTHER SIDE OF THE HILL

Introduction

"If there is any great secret in life, it lies in the ability to put yourself in the other persons place and to see things from their point of view – as well as your own" – Henry Ford

This ability to see things from another's point of view is especially critical when planning for and participating in a negotiation. Failure to take the other party's needs, interests and wants into consideration is the equivalent of "Bringing a knife to a gunfight" and risking the loss of significant value to your organisation. Why would the other party in a negotiation agree your proposals if it was not getting its own interests met?

This chapter builds on the preparation, objective setting and planning which has been carried from our own perspective and looks in practical terms at what we need to do to really understand how things look from the point of view of the other party in the negotiation. We will consider the information we need to gather to gain a realistic picture of what their interests might be, where we might get that information and how best to utilise it to anticipate potential roadblocks on the journey to agreement.

The two most difficult questions for most negotiators are ones they should ask themselves. These are "Where do I open?" and "When do I walk away?" It makes good commercial sense to consider also "Where will they open?" and "When will they walk away?" It is important to remember that in general we do not go into a commercial negotiation just for the sake of it, we and the other party are trying to obtain a competitive advantage and there are a number of different ways to achieve this. The most appropriate way to attain this advantage will depend on several key drivers for both sides. It will depend on how collaboration or competition is perceived within the relevant organisations, the skill of the negotiators on both sides and the relative balance of negotiating power between the parties.

We all make assumptions however it is dangerous to rely on them. How often have you heard phrases such as:

- They will never go for that

- They get much more training than we do
- This will be a pretty simple job
- It's obvious what their approach will be

Sometimes we are too optimistic, at other times we are far too defeatist and in a lot of cases we just get it wrong. It is worthwhile remembering the story of Bata shoes in Africa.

Several shoe companies in the late 19th century carried out assessments of the potential market in Africa. Typically the reports came back with something along the lines of "Nobody wears shoes here, no market for our product". The report from the Bata Shoes representative said "Nobody wears shoes here, huge market for our products". Bata went on to build a reputation as "The Shoes of Africa". Sometimes even when we have the same information, it is the analysis and interpretation of that data which can give us a competitive edge. Seeing something in a slightly different way from others and building a case to persuade others that your vision is one they can buy into.

Even where we end up being proved correct in our assumptions it is rarely wrong to at least question or test them. In planning for a negotiation there is a lot data about the other party which we can find out in advance. There will also be data that we cannot find out in advance, but we can at least plan how to access that information once negotiations commence. One assumption it is safe to make is that they will be trying to find out the same sort of information regarding our organisation. If a deal does not meet the interests, needs and wants of the other party why would they do the deal? If we do not know what the interests of the other party are, how likely is it we will satisfy them? If we do not know what they are now, we need to find out.

Getting a good understanding of what is important to the other party at the organisational level is crucial as it allows you to:

- Determine what you have that is of value to them, which is easy for you to trade
- Develop deals that acceptably satisfy the other party's interests, whilst providing added value to your own organisation
- Explore more creative and innovative solutions you may not have considered otherwise
- Avoid timewasting through persevering with proposals which have little chance of being considered
- Understand the impact of proposals you were considering making
- Identify unexpected complexity

Successful negotiations involve the parties identifying some common ground or interests.

As identified by Gavin Kennedy there is a reason why restaurants offer a bottle of House Wine to compensate for a poor customer experience. The concession is easy for them to make as they value the wine at the price, they pay wholesale (not very much) the customer sees the price on the wine list (pretty expensive). Customer and restaurant both see this as win/ win as it meets their interests.

It makes little sense to leave this till a negotiation is underway and a wealth of information about where the other party's interests and ours might coincide, is freely available and in the public domain. This could be from sources such as Companies House, published report and accounts or articles in the press and Social Media.

- What is their organisation vision / mission etc?
- What are their core values?
- What are their standard terms and conditions with customers / suppliers?
- What do we know about their products?
- Do they use conformance or performance specifications?
- What published policies do we know about?
- What do we know about the culture of the other party?
- What is their approach to Long term partnership relationships?
- What are their policies regarding Environment, Ethics etc?
- Over and above the published information there will be information that we can pick up or have already picked up because of previous dealings we have had or other members of our network have had.
- What are the KPIs for their organisation?
- What are the limits of authority of their negotiators?
- What service levels do they offer internally?
- Would they prefer a short term or long-term relationship?
- Would they prefer a win / win or win/ lose outcome?

Information at the organisational level is important and can be supplemented with information regarding the individuals who might be negotiating on their behalf as well as key customers, competitors and suppliers.

- Information at the individual level allows us to:
- Understand the motivators for key individuals
- Identify the forces pushing them towards or away from a deal with us
- Foresee proposals they might make and prepare possible responses

- Overcome objections they might make to our proposals
- Make suggestions for inclusion on project teams

Carrying out research on individuals within their organisation as well as thinking in advance about their key external stakeholders is likely to reveal:

- Who within their organisation do we have strong relationships with?
- Who within their organisation might have the power to block an agreement?
- What do we know about the individuals who will negotiate for the other party?
- If negotiation team involved, what do we know about personalities, authority and roles
- What do we know about their organisational politics?
- Who are their customers?
- What service levels do they offer to other customers?
- Who else in their industry can you talk to?
- Who in our company has worked with them before?
- Who are their key suppliers?
- What do we know about their costing methodology?
- What are normal margins in their industry? Do they see themselves as a premium or bargain brand in that market?
- Who are their key competitors? What prices do their competitors charge?
- How important are we to them as a customer / supplier?
- What percentage of their turnover do we represent?

There are numerous sources of information which can be accessed in a legal and ethical way to build up a picture of what is acceptable to them, what is desirable to them as well as realising what sort of offers, approaches and tactics are likely to be counterproductive. What seems like prudent and practical common sense to one company might seem like an aggressive attack to another. By asking questions similar to (but not limited to) those above we can build a picture of who else can meet their interests, if they can satisfy their interests through internal means and who they are trying to gain a competitive advantage over.

At an individual level, an appreciation of motivating and constraining forces, of personal preferences with regard to communication and influencing style and information regarding achievements and challenges of the individual help us to take practical steps to shape our approach to building rapport and moving toward agreement. It also helps if we can understand the internal organisational political situation within their company. Which departmental customers wield the most influence? Sales? Production? Finance? How can we use this information to our advantage?

A key consideration in any negotiation is power. Power can be financial, intellectual or moral, it can be real, or it can be perceived. An example of power in a negotiation is the ability to say, "This deal does not make good business sense for our organisation, we are walking away from it." This puts you in a position of power if you have an alternative you can rely on as a backup plan. This might be to carry out the task or project, yourself, get another partner to do it for you or to postpone the decision to sometime in the future. If you have no such backup plan rather than being in a position of power, you are in a position of weakness.

Realising that working out what your alternative might be is good practice, it follows that we should expect the other party to do the same. We should therefore try to anticipate both where they will open the negotiation and where they will prefer their backup plan. Harvard Business School call this walk-away position the BATNA (Best Alternative to a Negotiated Agreement).

Doing some basic research into their opening position and their BATNA will enable you to:

- Understand the range of choices they have for satisfying their interests, this will help you identify the basic hoops your proposal will need to get through in order to get them to agree it.
- Depending on findings you might make your own BATNA more optimistic or cautious as a result.
- Identify where they are playing hardball regarding what is acceptable so you can guard against unnecessary concessions.
- Develop arguments that make their walk-away alternative look less attractive to them, which will consequently make your proposal look more attractive to them and increase their likelihood of accepting it.
- Think about subtle ways to frame discussion of their BATNA, which can once again make your proposal look more attractive by comparison.
- Avoid situations where deadlock is inevitable as you have no space to move.

Tools

In conjunction with brainstorming techniques there are a number of tools and techniques which we can utilise to give us an indication about the options open to the other party. These might include carrying out STEEPLE analysis and SWOT analysis from their point of view to identify some of the bigger picture issues they face. What are the pressures they face to do a deal? What are their strengths, weaknesses opportunities and threats? How will these be manifested in the way they present their opening position and how hard will they fight to avoid having to go to their BATNA? This can be done in conjunction with doing a similar exercise for our own side. To a certain extent the process of planning for a negotiation could be likened to the Johari Window (below) a model created in 1955 by Joseph Luft and Harrington Ingham.

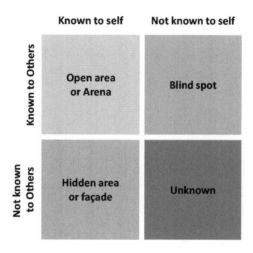

The Johari Window Model

Figure 1: Johari Window

The original model was largely used to allow people to better understand relationships between themselves and others. Using it as a practical negotiation tool allows us to consider what we know about the other party that they also know, to identify where we have information, they are not aware of that might constitute a blind spot. We can also look at information we have that we do not have access to but they might, as well as those factors which are apparently unknown to both parties.

Having carried out our assessment we should now have some ideas about what some of the information discussed is worth to both sides and seen some areas where there are potential trade-offs. Discussing information available to both parties might be a non-threatening way to open the negotiation and set the scene for exploring some more contentious and less obvious fields. If we can identify known areas where we have something in common, we can think about using this as a starting point. Once we have agreed on one issue, it becomes easier to agree on others. We have begun to create a climate where both sides see agreement is possible and have actually already made an investment of time and energy in moving in that direction.

Authority

Anyone who has been involved with buying double glazing for their house will know that the salesperson who comes to your house will have limited authority. Before you get to the best available deal you may have to endure numerous conversations involving phrases like "I will need to phone my boss to see what he/she says about that".

You may even have to wait for a day or two before you get a call back to let you that the last offer you made is now deemed acceptable (since you did not call them up to offer more). Organisations limit authority in this way because they know it works. If you are on the receiving end of this it can however be quite frustrating and it makes sense to establish up front exactly what authority the other party has to accept a deal.

Knowing the other side's authority to commit gives you the ability to:

- Avoid making substantive concessions which cannot be reciprocated.
- Involve only appropriate key decision-makers, so speeding up the negotiation process.
- Optimise the escalation process if needed
- Decide which models could help your negotiation counterpart in their internal negotiations with stakeholders.
- Evaluate how you are progressing and facilitate communications with your stakeholders

In practical terms it is worthwhile taking the following into consideration when clarifying authority and decision-making responsibility:

1. Build a "Clarification of authority "step into the negotiation agenda
2. Based on organisation chart or previous history, who will be responsible for signing off on their side?
3. Develop questions / proposals to establish who / how sign off will happen

Questions

It is tempting to think that questions only come into play when negotiation has started. If we leave it till then, the questions we ask are likely to be woolly, vague and unfocused. A successful negotiator will consider what information they have? What information they lack? And develop questions possibly in conjunction with the rest of the negotiation team or key stakeholders that will elicit key information from the other party.

In addition to formulating powerful questions focused on seeing things from the other side's point of view, we should be asking some questions of ourselves.

- What questions might they ask us?
- How do we respond to their questions?
- What if...?
- What questions would we find difficult to answer?
- What questions do we positively want them to ask us?
- How can we create an opening in the negotiation to allow them to ask us these questions?

In any negotiation if you are in doubt as to what to do, the answer is generally a question. The more we can prepare, even if we do not need to ask them, the better.

"Do not criticise someone until you walk a mile in their shoes. That way, when they find out, you are a mile away and you have their shoes." – Steve Martin.

The quote by Steve Martin is a humorous take on what is assumed to be a Native American proverb which did not include the second sentence. The original version maybe had more to say about the importance of trying to appreciate the forces that affect another person, but I like the way Steve Martin's version includes an element of balancing risk and reward which seems highly relevant when it comes to negotiation.

Chapter Summary

In this chapter we considered:

- The importance of looking at things from the other party's point of view and how critical it is to focus on the real interests of the other party rather than relying on assumptions
- What information we need to look for at the organisational level to get clues about what those interests might be
- What information at the individual level can inform our thinking on the needs of the other party
- Some practical steps to assess the potential opening position and BATNA

from the other point of view and how we might react to a range of possibilities.

- How we might prepare powerful questions to uncover interests and needs of the other party and anticipate the questions they will ask us.

Case Study

Alice Burns and Tony Ransom are consultants for 151 Services ltd who provide a range of construction services. Their department specialises in sports stadium roofing and given the vicissitudes of the British climate they are kept very busy.

Alice and Tony have a negotiation scheduled with the directors of Oldtown Athletic, a well-established top-level football team.

The team has had some well publicised problems in recent times including safety concerns about the iconic but ageing stadium with its safety certificate due for renewal. There are rumours about the long-term financial viability of the club though Callum Dunlop the Managing Director has insisted in the press that finances are in a robust condition. Money from season ticket sales will not be available however for another four months. The team are currently performing well though there is pressure from the fans for investment to be made in strengthening the team.

151 have identified that the Main Stand roof supports are in a poor condition and to even meet the minimum standards to have the safety certificate renewed will cost £2m. To really address all of the safety issues identified will be in the region of £10m and might involve playing matches away from home for a couple of months.

Alice is feeling confident, "It's obvious what their interests are, and they have no option".

Tony is a bit more cautious and wonders if they are missing something.

Task

How would you advise Alice and Tony regarding the interests and needs of their customer?

CHAPTER 5 | INITIAL MEETING – SETTING THE SCENE

Introduction

"The No. 1 rule in any negotiation is don't take yourself hostage. People do this to themselves all the time by being desperate for 'yes' or afraid of 'no,' so they don't ask for what they really want. Instead, they ask for what they can realistically get. I've heard many people say, 'Well, that's a non-starter, so we won't even bring it up.'" – Christopher Voss

In this chapter we look at strategies to avoid taking ourselves hostage, explore the importance the initial meeting and how spending the time in getting to relate to the other party can pay huge dividends later. We will discuss how to create an environment which is conducive to both parties being open to hearing the ideas and proposals of the other, look at a range of different approaches to making a powerful start to the negotiation and how we can contribute to clear, fair, rules of engagement.

In running several Negotiation courses over the years, I have observed how often participants at the planning stage make statements such as: "Let's cut straight to the chase, no wasting time on any pleasantries". I soon learned that this approach often leads to conflict and deadlock.

Getting the atmosphere right

To illustrate what we mean, let me share a story from our own personal experience of how the initial contact played a part in achieving a surprising outcome. In bidding for some work for a well-known airline, we arrived nice and early and were welcomed in by a couple of the people we would be pitching to.

They were waiting on their colleague to arrive. We settled down with them had some coffee and biscuits and had a general chat with them. Things were very relaxed, and we seemed to hit it off quite well and they even laughed at couple of our poor jokes. Eventually their colleague made an appearance and we moved into the room where the presentation was to take place.

As part of our presentation the consultant had an opening question asking how long it took to make a first impression. One of the business managers replied, "About 30 seconds actually". "So maybe you have already made your mind up," he said. "Don't feel you have to listen to the whole presentation if you want to give me the business anyway". (He did say it in a slightly jokey manner just in case). He glanced at his colleague who said "I suppose he does recognise a buying signal when he sees it". "OK You're in."

Obviously, we were delighted, however we did realise that these opportunities do not come along every day of the week. It did illustrate for us the importance of preparing carefully. We had the full presentation ready if he had just laughed at the suggestion. It just seemed at the time that the groundwork had already been done prior to coming into the conference room from the office. I suppose the chat in the office was the initial meeting and where the relaxed climate had been created that gave them some reassurance that we knew what we were talking about. It also gave us the confidence to ask for more than we really thought was achievable as "If you don't ask you don't get". There were indications from them that they were likely to be receptive to suggestions we might make.

The Map is not the Territory

Now in most commercial negotiations the result is not going to fall into your lap in the way that this one did for me. That does not mean you should expect failure, just that you might need to work a bit harder to achieve success. In any initial meeting with a client, with a supplier or an internal stakeholder you need to know what you are aiming for and to know how you can move the other party along the road to giving it to you.

In earlier chapters we explored concepts such:

* Setting objectives
* BATNA
* SWOT and PESTLE
* Identifying tradeables
* Putting yourself into their shoes
* Best and worst outcomes

Up to this point these were at best a rough map of the territory, at the initial meeting you are entering the actual territory. When we walk into a conference room, pick up the phone or switch on the video conferencing system we are getting a great opportunity to test some of the assumptions we have made to this point.

Agreeing an Agenda and "Rules of the Game"

Proposing an agenda can be useful in getting control of the commercial negotiation and help with the structuring of our case. We need to be careful in doing this as the agenda can turn out to be the first issue that we negotiate on. Whilst we might prefer to pursue our own agenda, we should ensure they feel they have an input and are being listened to. An agreed agenda is much more persuasive than an imposed agenda. If we can follow a pre-planned sequence of topics, that might be a good thing but not if it is at the expense of putting up barriers to movement with the other party. At this early stage it is also worth while agreeing "The rules of the game".

Not just what we will discuss but also testing our understanding about how we will work together, how we will resolve disputes, what authority each party must make decisions and what process we need to put in place for confirming any agreement we might reach. Giving some clarity on such issues might help us avoid falling into pitfalls such as those faced by the UK government in its Brexit negotiations in 2018.

Benefits of a Clear Agenda

- Provides structure for the discussions to follow
- Sets out the purpose of the commercial negotiation
- Ensures key issues of all parties are covered
- Limits discussion to relevant topics
- Allows a focused use of participants time
- Facilitates control if participants deviate
- Evaluation tool, we can measure if we have achieved what we agreed at outset

How an agenda is "Framed" can be crucial in getting a successful outcome. Framing is how we describe the situation or our agenda or our position to the other party. This is based partly on reality but partly on perception. If we understand that they have a view of the world or industry or negotiation, we can reflect that in the way we position our agenda with them. If we know they are very risk averse, we can focus on how it will remove risks. If they are very driven by the bottom line, we focus on how profitable it will be for them. Careful framing of your agenda can go a long way to ensuring that discussions can at least start productively) As part of the agenda setting exercise, it is wise to draw out what both sides are trying to achieve. (What good looks like) If this agreed upfront it can be used during the later stage to confirm that a Win /win deal is on the table.

In our planning for the commercial negotiation, we discussed identifying areas of common interest, if possible, we should try to get these discussed early. As there is common ground, we are more likely to be able to reach a quick resolution of these issues, this will build momentum, and give confidence to both parties that we can work together to resolve the other more contentious issues we still face. Once we have agreed on one issue, it is like making a deposit in a bank, we have invested in the negotiation. This means that further on in the negotiation we might reflect that we now have something to lose. We naturally fight harder to retain something we feel we worked hard for, so we try to find more creative ways to avoid deadlock.

Physical Logistics
If the commercial negotiation is going to a involve a face to face meeting and it is at our premises, this gives us even more opportunity to exercise some control over the physical environment. Factors such as seating arrangements, temperature, lighting, provision of refreshments and access to infrastructure such as Wi-Fi etc. can be adjusted to ensure we provide a comfortable experience for the participants. These variables can also be used in a manipulative way for short term advantage but if we want to develop a productive long-term relationship, this approach is unlikely to create the right atmosphere. Alison Wood Brooks in a *Harvard Business Review* article "Emotion and the Art of Negotiation" discussed how emotions such as anxiety, anger, disappointment and regret played a major part in determining the outcomes of commercial negotiations. Understanding and controlling your own emotions, recognising emotional signals from the other party and using emotional intelligence to build rapport is more likely to be successful if you pay attention to the emotional climate from the start as opposed to reacting in the middle of the negotiations. A certain amount of time needs to be allowed for "settling in", relating to the other participants on a human level and allowing nerves on both sides to dissipate.

Psychologically it is in our interest to focus not on our perceived weaknesses or why we "Need to make this deal" – instead we should concentrate on how they will be feeling and what pressure they could be under. Your role at this stage is remain calm, even if they appear to be extremely confident. Much better to be in detective mode, asking open questions to understand their position than to be in lecturer mode, giving them your thoughts views and opinions.

Rather than looking to "Win" the negotiation better seeking to understand their interests and showing them how you can facilitate those interests being met. To get "Buy in" from the other party takes skill in building rapport and demonstrating that you can empathise with their situation. As we are in uncharted territory it is wise to keep an open mind during the early stages of a commercial negotiation and avoid jumping to too many conclusions

How to Develop Rapport

Here are some best practices to facilitate the development of rapport between the parties, as used by professional negotiators.

- Pick safe topics for initial "Small talk"
- Don't be afraid to try out some humour but do be aware of the risk involved in this, you want to break the ice not create it.
- Develop awareness of non-verbal signals you might send out, reinforce deliberate ones and control inadvertent ones
- Can you demonstrate how your interests are in alignment with theirs?
- Let them see how much you value this relationship, build your likeability.
- Take responsibility for getting all the issues on the table at an early stage so there are no surprise Exocet missiles which blow the negotiation out of the water at the last minute.
- Keep asking questions, show you are interested.

Opening Gambits

In the early stages of this meeting each party will likely be trying to "Sound out" the other so in a sense you should expect a bit of positioning. If taking a superficial approach to commercial negotiation there is often a reluctance to make the first offer as there is a perception, that this risk giving away your "position".

In a long-term commercial negotiation if the parties really do have the potential to work together, we must start somewhere. This might involve making the opening offer and I do not believe we should be afraid of doing so. In the story in the earlier paragraph we saw how powerful a first impression can be, we should concentrate on making this impression a positive one.

One way to generate this positive impact is to take responsibility for getting things moving. By taking the initiative in this way. You appear to be decisive and to know what you want. Another advantage of making the first offer is the concept of "Anchoring" as outlined by Grant and Galinsky. If you make a strong optimistic offer, even though the other party may not like it he/she registers it and it affects their perception of what is reasonable. Research shows that they start to find positive reasons as to why you might be making that offer. As a result of this there is a tendency to "bracket" their offer closer to your opening and revise their aspirations downward.

Opening Moves

- Stress some common purpose and interest

- Frame your agenda to reflect their preferences
- Be optimistic, clear and positive
- All offers should be conditional
- They should be capable of being "Built on" to show flexibility
- Include at least a grain of realism to demonstrate credibility and generate interest
- Demonstrate confidence and
- Promote goodwill

By starting off optimistically we give ourselves some scope to move from our opening gambit with some credibility if we face a challenge from the other party. As having your opening offer accepted is relatively rare, we need to think of how we will respond to a rejection of our opening offer. Remaining calm, not taking any rejection too personally and asking sensible questions to clarify why they did not want to accept the offer, will pay dividends. If we make our offers at the early stage too firm, we run the risk of the other party feeling there is no scope for movement. Making the opening offer slightly tentative gives them an idea of where we are but indicates that if they were to offer us something of interest then a deal might be possible. "How about if you take on the risk for the initial period, we can support once the training period is complete" as opposed to "We need you to take on the risk initially, we cannot get involved till the training period is over."

In any successful negotiation both parties will be making proposals, how we handle those made by the other party will be just as important as those we make. Even if we do not like their proposals, we need to treat the individual making them with respect. The last thing we want to do is upset their emotional equilibrium when based on the facts, a deal is available. It is also easy to assume that their analysis of the situation is the same as ours, maybe they are feeling the pressure more and will offer us a better deal than we thought was possible. If this is the case it makes sense to keep an open mind and question their rationale for this offer, maybe they could improve it further. In saying that keeping an open mind is useful, bear in mind there might be some gambits the other party decides to employ. These could include

- Saying they have limited authority
- Take it or leave it
- Exaggerated claims
- Good cop, bad cop
- Asking for one-way concessions

- Setting out a series of "red lines"

When faced with these gambits we need to respond professionally and with respect, whilst at the same time communicating a strong signal that we understand the approach they are taking and are not fazed by it.

Best practice tips for receiving opening offers

- Listen carefully, they might offer more than you expected
- Be prepared to build on them rather than reject outright
- Avoid making an immediate counter offer, at least appear to consider their offer (they will be at their least receptive having just made their offer)
- Clarify and test for understanding if there is any ambiguity
- Use non-verbal signals to communicate emotion in a subtle manner
- Do not accept too quickly, if it seems too good to be true it probably is
- Look for common ground and encourage further movement

For successful commercial negotiations, I have stressed the importance of planning and explained some of the consequences of failing to do so. In this regard I can see that I have a lot in common with Sun Tzu who stated in *The Art of War* the memorable phrase:

"If you know the enemy and know yourself, you need not fear the result of a hundred battles. If you know yourself but not the enemy, for every victory gained you will also suffer a defeat. If you know neither the enemy nor yourself, you will succumb in every battle."

In a commercial negotiation we want to avoid losing every single battle, so we should do as much planning as is reasonably possible to understand the, needs, interests and drivers for all parties to the potential deal.

The Need for Flexibility

In the real world as opposed to the ideal world we often have less control than we would desire. There may be a situation where you did not even recognise that you would be negotiating until you were in the middle of it. This was the situation some colleagues found themselves in when working in Africa, running a training course to prepare learners for professional exams a month later. At the time they were running the event there was an industrial action taking place in the workplace. In the middle of their morning session they were interrupted by a group of singing and chanting union members with a megaphone who burst into the into classroom and told them, "You must leave".

They were a bit perplexed but attempted tried to find out the rationale for this action, by asking several questions. After a few minutes' discussion a lady at the back of the crowd of demonstrators, stated, "No need to worry, there will be no violence, no one is going to hurt you". Until she said that, the thought had never crossed their minds. Realising that the situation was getting slightly emotional it was agreed that they would evacuate the room but not right away.

They explained they felt obligated to learners as they felt responsible for preparing them for the upcoming exams. If they gave 15 minutes, then our colleagues would negotiate with the hotel next door and put together a plan with the delegates to run the afternoon session at the new location. As the exact timing of our departure was not of critical importance to the union, they were happy to agree to this as they had not lost face. The consultants had not just accepted their initial offer (or threat) and ultimately, they got their way, but we also managed to make an alternative arrangement.

The result was an afternoon session in the sunshine in the Terrace Bar by the swimming pool with some complementary soft drinks provided by the hotel management. The delegates felt that the relaxed atmosphere helped them absorb some key information and said they would be happy to do the same next day. Apparently some were sorry that the industrial dispute was resolved that afternoon. Although there was a successful outcome, our colleagues could not claim that they had prepared carefully for this initial meeting, as prior to the interruption they had no idea any negotiation would take place. In this case the initial meeting was the only meeting. In situations such as this you just need to be flexible, calm and try to clarify the situation as much as you can in the time available.

In most commercial negotiations, you are likely to have at least some notice that you will be carrying out the negotiation. Even if time is limited, you should still be able to give some consideration to what you want to achieve, how you will approach it, what your opening offer will be and where you think they will open. Think in advance of how you would prefer to structure the meeting, what you can do to build rapport with the other party and how you can create an environment where they are receptive to your ideas. As in all areas of commercial negotiations staying calm and behaving flexibly are key skills.

Chapter Summary
In this chapter we have considered:

- The importance of the initial meeting and its relevance in creating a good first impression

- how investing time in building rapport pays off in the longer term
- Identified benefits of having a clear agenda
- Examined some powerful opening gambits, how to use an opening offer to "Anchor "the other party.
- Described some common gambits the other party might utilise
- Looked at approaches to handling opening offers from the other party

---

Case Study

Startword Inc are new to the field of artificial Intelligence for "Robotic hotel services". CEO, Linda, believes there are huge opportunities for organisations who can come up with innovative ideas and anticipate what services and products will appeal to the modern Business and Leisure traveller.

Linda and her colleague Zhang from corporate procurement at Startword have been planning for the last week for an important negotiation with a key supplier Maid4U who have developed a room service robot, which can be programmed to deliver small items to hotel guests in their rooms. Linda is impressed with the current capabilities of this robot and wonders how some of its functionality might be utilised in other areas of a hotel operation such as the spa and bar.

Linda feels they are well prepared for this commercial negotiation as she has worked out a SWOT Analysis, set her objectives, has a BATNA clearly defined. She knows in detail the budget she must work with and has done a lot of work to understand the current specifications of the product they are set to discuss.

Linda and Zhang are due to meet with Ken and Yoon from Maid4u later this afternoon and are just having a last pre -negotiation meeting to finalise their approach. Linda is extremely confident: "Hi Zhang, let's get to it, I think we are in a really strong position, they will be desperate for the level of business we can put their way. I think we should take a hard line in the early stages, so they can see what they might be missing out on if they do not play ball. I notice there are a few weaknesses with their finance, I think we should focus on that, so they understand who is dominant in this relationship."

Zhang did not say much but Linda was aware he was looking at her in a slightly concerned way. "Something wrong Zhang?"

"Just wondered if an approach where we focused on what we had in common initially, might not allow the relationship to develop a bit more naturally," he said. "If we start off too aggressively, that might increase the chance of deadlock."

"Do we even know much about their negotiators? Maybe if we play our cards right, they will offer us more than we might ask for."

"I suppose it is a consideration," she said. "But to me we need to be in control, I suggest we start off with Finance, move on to Technical Specifications, then lead into Price and Quality Control."

"What if they have other ideas?" asked Zhang." I agree we need to discuss all these things but are you really saying if we cannot discuss them in that order, we will walk away from the deal?"

"I have a number of unanswered questions in my head at the moment." mused Zhang. "How important is the ongoing relationship to us? What sort of first impression do we want to make? What are the consequences if we make the wrong impression? What if they have a really good BATNA of their own?"

Task
How might this internal negotiation between Linda and Zhang be resolved?

CHAPTER 6 | DEVELOPING COMMERCIAL NEGOTIATION STRATEGIES AND TACTICS

Definition
A commercial negotiation strategy is a pre-determined approach or prepared plan of action to achieve a specific goal or objective to potentially find and make an agreement or contract in a commercial negotiation with another party or parties.

Tactics
Negotiation tactics are the methods used by negotiators to gain an advantage. Tactics can be deceptive and manipulative and are used to fulfil one party's goals. This makes many tactics in use 'win-lose' by nature.

Developing the Negotiation Strategy
There are many factors that need to be taken into consideration when developing the commercial negotiation strategy and deciding upon the desired outcomes from the commercial negotiation. These can include:

- The nature of the item or service, in terms of risk and value
- Current and future supply market conditions
- Relative bargaining positions of the buyer and the supplier
- Existing or desired relationship
- Risk and Value Classification

The DPSS Contract Risk and Value Classification Application is designed to enable organisations to determine the risk to value status of a new contract before taking it forward and this could influence the commercial negotiation strategy. The process, which is based upon the famous Kraljic model, involves the assessment of the inherent risks associated with goods or services. These risks include commercial impact, technology, supply market and people. Next, the value of the contract is input.

The outcome from the assessment is then displayed in the form of a Kraljic style matrix. In this case the analysis indicates this item or service is of critical importance and therefore a win/win style of commercial negotiation may be appropriate given the risks associated with win/lose.

Figure 1: Kraljic model

Strategic

In this case the analysis indicates this item or service is of critical importance and therefore a win/win style of commercial negotiation maybe appropriate given the risks associated with win/lose. Strategic contracts are those with the highest risk and of greatest strategic or commercial value to the organisation. The impact that success or failure within this contract setting will be highest and, in many cases have a very high positive and or negative impact on the performance of the organisation's objectives. To ensure success therefore the highest level of attention is paid to the commercial negotiation of such contracts.

Bottleneck

These are considered high risk and of low value within the organisation. The impact that of failure may be high and directly affect the performance of the organisation, yet the relative expenditure may be relatively small. These contracts are often critical support contracts without which the organisation cannot function or patented or original equipment manufacturers (OEM) but the relative investment may be quite low. Therefore, the issue is the cost of non-availability (CNA) suppliers are often aware of this and hold some power in such circumstances. This can influence the commercial negotiation strategy toward either win/win or lose/win to ensure supply.

Routine
Routine goods and services are considered low risk and of low value within the organisation. The impact that success or failure within this contract setting will have little positive or negative impact. In many cases these contracts live in markets where there is a high level of competition and where there are other suppliers who could fulfil the contractual obligations. In this situation commercial negotiations may not be required, and procurement can rely on market forces and competition to secure the most desirable outcome.

Leverage
Leverage goods and services are considered low risk but of high potential or value within the organisation. In such markets, there is often healthy competition and the organisation should look to exploit their buying power or volume through procurement activity to extract value. Constant focus on reducing costs or improving quality or on-time delivery. In this situation the commercial negotiation strategy could lean toward a more aggressive win/lose outcome, although even in leverage cases, the risk of adopting win/lose is still high.

Dealing with Large Multinational Suppliers
In some instances, market conditions, can have a direct effect upon commercial negotiation strategies, for example dealing with a limited number of powerful supplies. Ricky Baharwal states "The key characteristic in such deals is that the natural balance of power moves from buyer to supplier. Big suppliers know their market power and don't hesitate to flex their muscles to maintain the status quo. These conditions arise in markets for various reasons or a combination of factors which may influence supply chains. In some markets, most suppliers have been eliminated due to tight competition, giving the remainder significant clout in the market".

One strategy he recommends to overcome this is to consolidate demand. "Combining your companies spend into one contract/purchase order is not only a logical way to spend, but is also an effective way to boost your corporate commercial negotiation power. The only caveat is that you need be able to collaborate internally to assess the total demand across the business".

Professor Jim Norton states, "The exponential growth of technology and data can be useful for procurement, but also has destructive potential." He goes on to say that technology can already "change the balance of power" in purchasing relationships and commercial negotiations by allowing companies to aggregate their buying or selling power. However, he said misusing e-commerce to drive down price had the potential to harm supplier relationships. This could also affect commercial negotiations and encourage a more win/lose style commercial negotiations in certain sectors.

Types of Negotiation Strategy

We can classify commercial negotiation strategies under two broad headings: win/win and win/lose:

Win/Win

These are characterised by integrative, collaborative, win/win, interest based, mutual gain and principled approached to commercial negotiations. All these styles focus on two or more issues to be negotiated, not just price. They often involve an agreement process that better integrates the aims and goals of all the involved negotiating parties through creative and collaborative problem solving.

This type of principled or win/win commercial negotiations is a concept that is based on the work of Roger Fisher and Bill Ury. This approach to commercial negotiation focuses on the interests of the parties and emphasizes conflict management and conflict resolution. The key elements of Principled include:

- Separate people from the problem being negotiated. Issues should be decided on their merits.
- Focus on the negotiating parties' interests, not their positions. The underlying interests or motivations that drive individuals in a commercial negotiation are often quite similar.
- Generate different options for mutual gain
- Base the outcome from a principled commercial negotiation session on objective criteria.

The Advantages of Win/win Style Commercial Negotiations

There is a high degree of presumed flexibility on both sides and a willingness to cooperate and collaborate to achieve a mutually acceptable outcome. Therefore, this type of commercial negotiation tends to be constructive and time efficient, given that both sides want to reach a sustainable agreement. This method of commercial negotiation provides a more effective alternative to positional bargaining. The win/win approach permits both sides to reach for a gradual consensus, efficiently and amicably.

Win/Win Risks

Adopting a win/win approach can expose either side to several significant risks. Over-dependence on few sources and vulnerability if problems occur. Costs of integration and high switching costs in event of problems. Vulnerability of intellectual property, confidential information, due to sharing info and may set a precedent for 'soft' bargaining target.

George Lucas wanted to sell his company, but also maintain his creative legacy. Walt Disney Chairman Robert Iger and Lucas conducted these principled win/win commercial negotiations personally. The Disney Corporation promised to begin producing and releasing new films in the Star Wars franchise every two or three years.

The acquisition even included a detailed script treatment for the next three Star Wars films. Speaking of Lucas' decision to hand over his creative legacy to Disney, Iger said "There was a lot of trust there."

Win/Lose

Whereas distributive, positional, bargaining, win-lose and sum zero commercial negotiation strategies tend to focus on a single issue to be negotiated. The single issue often involves price and frequently relates to the bargaining approach to the process of commercial negotiation.

This type commercial negotiation strategy usually involves holding on to a fixed idea, or position, of what you want and arguing for it and it alone, regardless of any underlying interests. Andy Brown of PMMS states "When you get to the heart of the commercial negotiation your objective is to move the other parties away from their position, while standing firm on your own" – this would seem to endorse a win/lose approach.

The advantages of win lose can include competitive advantage as the negotiator is targeted with obtaining their objectives to the detriment of the other party's. Negotiations are very focused and maybe more appropriate to leverage or transactional situations. Win-lose often perceived as a powerful perspective and position.

Win/Lose Risks

There are also significant risks related to win/lose. Loss of opportunity for added value, innovation from collaboration with suppliers. There will be no preferential relationship or supply in event of scarcity or disruption. We may win on price, but loose in terms of quality, delivery and service. Win/lose tends to set an adversarial precedent for all future commercial negotiations, even when circumstance dictate that win/win would be more appropriate.

Framing

"A means to process and organise information." A frame provides a perspective of the problems or issues for a decision maker. Using a framework can allow us to consider all potential gains and losses and available options for any situation. This framing is sometimes referred to as "Half Empty v Half Full" and positive and negative "spin". The aim is the change the perception of a situation from bad to less bad, rather than from bad to good.

For example, we are discussing with a supplier the need to reduce our requirements. In plan A, we will save one your 3 contracts and will save 2000 jobs. Plan B plan will result in the loss of 2 contracts and the loss of 4000 jobs. Same outcome, but a positive perspective.

Negotiation Tactics and Ploys

There are many commercial negotiation tactics and ploys, although many are associated with win/lose style commercial negotiations, they have their place in many commercial negotiation situations. However, there is a fine line between tactics and "tricks" and we must be careful not to cross that line or indeed, allow the other side to cross it. We have covered these tactics more from the perspective of not being tricked by them, rather than advocating their general use. A full list of typical commercial negotiation tactics can be found on the internet http://changingminds.org/disciplines/commercial negotiation/tactics/tactics.htm

We have chosen a few examples to highlight:

Salami

Asking for several small concessions, so that as the commercial negotiation progresses, these become cumulatively significant, rather than demanding from the outset major concessions that maybe rejected out of hand by the other side.

To counter this tactic, keep careful track of these concessions and set a limit. It is also advisable to "condition" the supplier by often repeating that the final agreement is final.

Boil the frog

The analogy is placing a frog in hot water (hostile environment) he will react defensively and hop out. If, however the water is warm and tepid, he will feel safe and secure. The heat can then be slowly increased until the poor frog (or the other side) is cooked. In other words, the other side will start gently and gradually racket up the pressure.

To counter this tactic by being wary of overly soft and personal opening to the negotiations, keep alert to any subtle changes in tone and nuance, especially as the negotiations start to deal with contentious issues.

Stairway to Agreement

This is also based upon creating a very positive and constructive atmosphere, the focus at the beginning of the commercial negotiation will be on the points of agreement. For example, the buyer may send out lots of "buy" signals, agreeing to delivery dates, packaging, payment terms etc and the supplier becomes confident that he will achieve his objective, but then the buyer will ask for his major concession, say a 20% cut in the price. The psychology of this is that having made so much progress on some many points, the other side will concede to get closure.

To counter this tactic be wary of these "positive" signals and intervene with your own reality checks by asking what the major concession in advance is of reaching that point.

Russian Front

In World War II, being sent to the Russian Front was almost a guaranteed death sentence. Therefore, the tactic is to highlight the mutual risks to both sides by not reaching an agreement and thus leverage some concessions.

No Cost Concession

This is the simple (but effective) tactic of having several "concessions" to offer the other side, often with dramatic effect, that have no real cost implication. For example, one side may offer some additional service that has perceived value to the other side but has no cost implications. In return however the concession is expected to be reciprocated.

Ace in the Hole

This is the ploy of holding back something of value to the other side until the appropriate moment, for example keeping back that contract could be extended if a significant concession could be given by the other side or asking for the price of one and then later asking for the price of the full order.

To counter, you need to ask the supplier, at the appropriate moment if they are keeping anything back. This will put them into a difficult position, if indeed that we their intended tactic. They can hardly keep their integrity and credibility if they suddenly then pull out their ace in the hole card.

Snow Job

This is the tactic of blinding the opposition with facts and figures, options, timelines and data. The idea is to create confusion in the mind of the other side, as they attempt to work out the implications of these numerous options and therefore could encourage to accept an offer that suits the other side. To counter: this is when effective pre-negotiation preparation comes into its own and you can counter the supplier's facts and figures with your own and your previous analysis of the relative bargaining positions. It is also a counter to pose your questions upon the supplier in a role reversal.

Good cop/bad cop – this where the negotiators project a demeanour of one being very reasonable and has developed a goof rapport with the other side and displays empathy. Whilst his or her co negotiator appears aggressive, unreasonable and inflexible. The other party will tend to focus on the good cop and will endeavour to slide line the bad cop. The good cop will then seek concessions to "placate" the bad cop.

Silence – this is where one party does not respond to an offer or counter offer and the other side feel the need to fill the gap with a concession to re-engage and/or reconnect with the buyer or seller.

The Need to Share Information

Adam Grant and Adam Galinsky of North Western University state that commercial negotiators often approach commercial negotiation very guarded and wary of showing positions. However, as Grant points out, people tend to be matchers and "follow the norm of reciprocity, responding in kind to how we treat them." If we want to be trusted, we must first offer it. Studies have shown that revealing some information, even when it's unrelated to the commercial negotiation, increases the outcome.

Rank order your priorities

Grant recommends rank ordering. His research shows that negotiators can achieve better outcomes by ranking and leaving all the issues on the table and being transparent about it. That way both parties can compare their rankings and determine what the full set of options really are. Therefore we should go in knowing our target price and our walkaway terms.

Emotional Intelligence in Commercial Negotiations

Emotions that are often used in negotiation processes are guilt, anger and fear. These emotional 'buttons' can be pushed by a skilled operator to manipulate and manoeuvre the other party into an unfavourable position. They might use emotive language such as: "You promised me a better price in this round of negotiation and you are now letting me down," or "I will need to reduce some of my workforce if you keep me to these rates".

This has the effect of making the person feel guilty and could soften their approach. The counter position to guilt is acceptance. Once the guilt (whether justified or the opposite) is accepted, it loses its power and its influence, too. For example, you could answer the original statement with: "Yes, you are right to be upset but circumstances have changed." By accepting your guilt, you disarm the negotiator who is using it.

Keep Calm in the Face of Anger

Next comes anger and aggression. Some negotiators are very good at adopting an intimidating posture, using both their voice and body language. This could include invading your personal space, feigning exasperation, or banging fists on the desk, among a multitude of others. This tactic has potentially two outcomes. Either the other side is bullied into accepting the terms, or they too will react with anger and aggression of their own.

The skilled negotiator is never really angry, it is 'play acting', therefore their thought process is clear, and their judgement is unimpaired, although the victim is truly angry and may not be thinking rationally. The counter to this tactic is to remain calm and cool, backed up by silence – the aggressor relies upon a reaction to add fuel to the fire.

Don't be Afraid of Threats

The final ploy in this trio is fear and threats. These are statements such as: "If you do not sign today, I may not be able to meet your requirements," or "What would your end user say if you cannot secure the materials? I would not like to be in your shoes."

The counter to fear and threats is to be brave and to call their bluff. In most cases, these threats are empty, and our fears are unfounded. You should respond with: "I think I can deal with my stakeholders, I have worked with them for many years"; "I am prepared to take that risk"; or even, "You could be right, maybe I need to look for an alternative source."

The use of these powerful human emotions is traditionally associated in negotiations where there is a clear winner and loser, but that is not to say that they are not used or used but albeit in a subtler way, in all forms of negotiation and in many different contexts.

The Seven Tactics of Influence

The Seven Tactics of Influence were identified by Kipnis et al. (1980) Exchange and sanctions lead to compliance because the target is provided an incentive to change her behaviour. For example, the target may be given something in return for compliance (exchange) or be threatened with punishment for non-compliance (sanctions). Reason and assertiveness lead to compliance because the target's information set is changed. For example, the target may be given additional information to bolster the influencer's argument (reason) or be forced to consider more carefully the arguments already made (assertiveness). Tactics (coalition, ingratiation, and higher authority) entail a hybrid approach in which both incentives and information may be altered. When the influencer builds a coalition, the target's alternative to compliance may be worsened (incentive); at the same time, the existence of a coalition may suggest that the influencer's argument has merit (information).

If ingratiation increases the degree to which the target likes the influencer, this creates additional incentives to comply; ingratiation may also affect information by suggesting that the influencer has the target's best interest in mind.

Finally, appeals to a higher authority can change both the incentive to comply ("do this or else") and also the perceived reasonableness of the demand ("the boss says this is a good idea").

Chapter Summary

In this chapter we have considered:

- How to develop a robust negotiation strategy
- The role of risk and value classification in the development of negotiation strategies
- A range of typical negotiation tactics and ploys
- Evaluation of win/win, win/lose and lose/win style negotiation and the relative risks and benefit
- The concept of framing

Case Study

Torch Consultants are a group of engineering consultants, based in London. The company has recently secured a contract for the supply of a team of consultants to assist in the development of a technical scope of work for the new gas plant turnkey contract for Allied Oil and Gas plc. Part of the contract includes attending a series of meetings with the key stakeholders at the various sites around the UK.

These are considered by Allied to be very important events. A meeting is planned for the 15th July at 10am. Two consultants from Torch are due to attend. By chance, this meeting will also be attended by the CEO of Allied – Ms Alison Dache.

Due to a family crisis, one of the consultants does not make the meeting and the other one is late by one hour, due to local traffic. Alison is very angry at this unprofessional behaviour and informs the consultants that she intends to terminate the whole contract, with immediate effect and will make a claim for her wasted time, given that this critical event has not been properly resourced by Torch. The consultants have asked for a meeting to try and negotiate the continuation of the contract.

Task

What would your most and least desirable outcomes your commercial negotiation and what would your strategy be?

CHAPTER 7 | THE "MAIN" EVENT – CONDUCTING THE NEGOTIATIONS

Introduction

In this chapter, we will look at the actual commercial negotiation itself, consider the psychology of the participants and how it influences or even completely determines the outcomes for the parties involved. We will look at the communication skills that are needed to facilitate the optimum result for the participants, and how successful negotiators can persuade and influence the other party in a commercial negotiation even when the odds seem stacked against them. If you could negotiate a 5% improvement on every deal, how much of a hero would you be? On the other side of the coin when commercial negotiations such as that between Apple and Samsung go wrong, the parties can end up in court with liabilities of $409 million.

In earlier chapters, we have discussed the various phases of a commercial negotiation and looked at some of the activities that are involved in each. In our planning for this event we will already have gathered information, carried out benchmarking, identified variables and agreed our mandate with key stakeholders. We have looked at several factors from our perspective and the perspective of the other side and we have given serious thought to the logistical issues involved in a commercial negotiation. All this planning is essential though it is worth bearing in mind that "A battle plan never survives contact with the enemy" – Von Moltke. This is not to infer that the negotiation will be an adversarial one however there comes a time for action and the plan must be put into action in the real world. At this point it is worth asking yourself:

- What state of mind do you want to be in?
- What state of mind would you want the other person to be in?
- What can you do to make both, realities?

The Positional Approach

Our state of mind when entering into commercial negotiations might vary depending on whether we are taking a "Positional" approach to negotiation or a "Principled approach.

"When the final result is expected to be a compromise, it is often prudent to start from an extreme position." – John Maynard Keynes *(The Economic Consequences of the Peace)*

In taking a Positional Approach the negotiator will decide on a position prior to the start of the negotiation and try to get a deal as close to that as possible. It is likely that the negotiator using this approach will try to "Condition" the other party through exaggerated claims and bluffs with little attempt to explore alternative outcomes.

The downside of the positional approach is that it tends to trigger a reciprocal approach by the other party and several beneficial outcomes are never even discussed as no-one wants to be perceived as soft or naïve. The mind-set when entering a positional negotiation is like that of a poker player.

There may be situations where a positional approach is appropriate, particularly if it is unlikely to result in a long-term relationship. In more complex commercial negotiations however, especially those which will necessitate ongoing collaboration, a principled approach is likely to be more fruitful.

The Principled Approach

The principled approach to commercial negotiations involves taking a stance that both parties have interests in common and if we work hard at uncovering the real needs and interests of the other party it is possible to find a solution that addresses these interests. Even if this does not happen, we have a better understanding of why such a deal is not a good one for both parties on this occasion and keep the relationship and communication channels open for opportunities in the future.

The psychology of someone utilising a principled approach is that of an open-minded problem solver. In a principled negotiation, there are real benefits to being optimistic and open to possibilities. "Every man takes the limits of his own field of vision for the limits of the world." – Arthur Schopenhauer *(Studies in Pessimism: The Essays)*

There may be circumstance when the benefits of a principled approach in terms of flexibility, building a relationship and solving problems can be outweighed by the drawbacks of the time it takes to uncover and meet real needs and by the additional complexity introduced by trying to balance several different variables.

The good news is that there are an endless range of possibilities when it comes to structuring commercial negotiations, as it is easy to find different ways to describe the same basic things. To keep things on a practical level we can look at four main stages.

1. Opening
2. Discussion and debate
3. Threat of deadlock
4. Agreement and close

Opening

In Chapter 4 we mentioned Johari window and the benefits of working to maximise the open area. In the early stages of a commercial negotiation it is easy to fall prey to the temptation to "Just get on with it". Taking this approach seems like the easy way out and a great way to save time. It can also lead to some obvious common interests not being revealed, the atmosphere seeming a little "frosty" and each party taking a relatively defensive approach to the other. By focusing on the relationship, disclosing some personal information from our side and seeking reciprocal behaviour from them we can start to establish some sort of rapport, put the other party at ease and let them see that we do not view this negotiation as a war of attrition.

It makes sense in this opening stage to:

- Refer to areas where we have common interests
- Agree the working relationship, build rapport
- Put our cards on the table regarding our preferred agenda
- Give them the opportunity to outline their preferred agenda
- Ask a ton of questions, get all the issues on the table
- Ascertain the gap between the parties
- Agree a way forward that suits both parties.

This stage of the negotiation may not be the first time the parties have communicated as there will have been exchanges of documents or analysis of Social Media prior to the meeting. It might however be the first face to face encounter and as such it is important to weigh up the impression you want to have on the other party. All communication has a context and factors such which party is the initiator or the responder can colour perceptions of strength and risk and whether they want to do business with your organisation. You are much more likely to achieve success in commercial negotiations if you are assertive rather than aggressive or passive. In our planning, we have identified our most desirable outcome and it seems logical that if that is what we want to achieve it would make no sense at all not to ask for it.

By making an initial optimistic but justifiable opening offer we can influence the other party and "Anchor" that in their minds (see Tversky and Kahneman)

We must however, if we desire credibility, be able to justify why we think it is reasonable to ask for it. We should not expect they will automatically agree with our analysis. We should listen carefully to the reasons they put forward as to why they do not agree.

At this stage, we start to make assumptions and judgements about the other party and if we do this too hurriedly there can be severe consequences. "They cause us to trust people who are deceptive. They cause us to undervalue how much certain people – who may be more competent than we think – could help us." Amy J.C. Cuddy, *Harvard Business Review.*

It is helpful in this early stage to be slightly tentative with any proposals.

So "How would you feel about a ratio of something like 7:3?" is more beneficial than "7:3 take it or leave it", there is a chance the other party feels fine about a 7:3 ratio but the door is still open even if they do not. If they seem keen to accept 7:3, can you build on it to get more? If you make your offers too "Take it or leave it" at this early stage, you may not get much further and you can antagonise the other party. It is better to get all the issues on the table rather than keeping key issues "Up your sleeve" for later. Do not be afraid to ask, "Is there anything else?" The time taken in this opening stage will depend on what is at stake and the complexity of the issues involved and it might be worthwhile considering if there should be a break for both parties to consider what they have learned from it.

Discussion and Debate
When the parties have satisfied themselves that they are clear on what they are negotiating about, the commercial negotiation will move from the "settling in and getting informed" stage to discussing how the parties can move from initial start points. In some cases, this will be formally signposted, in others we only realise we are there when we feel upset that they have rejected our "Very reasonable offers".

In this stage of the commercial negotiation we are going to be trying to persuade and influence the other party to move in our direction and there are a variety of verbal and non-verbal approaches that can be used in combination to achieve this end. No single method will work every time, but the skilled negotiator can pick up signals from their counterpart which reveals something about how they try to influence others.

Logic
Most people think they are logical, and they assume that other people share their sense of what is logical and will therefore be influenced in the same way that they are. If we think of logic as an influencing technique based on using facts,

evidence, numbers and reason, we consequently feel we are on safe ground as no one can argue with facts. Unfortunately for these people there are others who find this approach, boring, intimidating and unengaging and switch off when faced with it.

If you are one of these people who get bored by it you still need to influence people who prefer logic, so need to have evidence, facts and numbers to back up proposals and be prepared to explain your reasoning. In a commercial negotiation, it is important to understand costs, specifications, markets and resources. Edward de Bono coined the phrase "Logic Bubble" to explain how we see things from our own perspective and can assume people with a different perception of the scenario are ill informed or stubborn or stupid. It is important to recognise that if they see things from a different perspective, we need to question why that is? So, a logical approach to influencing the other party cannot be just about explaining our logic but should also be about getting them to explain theirs. This allows us to reveal deficits in the evidence for their view.

Reflection
Reflective behaviour involves letting the other party see how their offer appears to our side. Taking an element of what they have offered or threatened allows the other party to re-evaluate what they have said or done and consider if they can amend it. "So, there are legal reasons that prevent you from licensing us in the way you licence three of our competitors?" "What margin would you expect us to make in that situation?"

Assertion and Assertiveness
Assertion is sometimes known as the broken record technique, where you "Stick to your guns" and repeat what you want till the other side caves in. If using assertion, it is important that weak language does not creep into your vocabulary. Phrases such as "I know it seems a lot to ask" or "I hate doing this but…" are likely to undermine the whole approach and make it easier for the other side to disagree.

There might be situations where assertion is needed, particularly in near deadlock situations but overuse can lead to a perception of inflexibility. Assertiveness is a mode of communication that sits between passivity and aggression. It is about making your case strongly without denigrating the other party. Assertiveness is not about talking down to people or feeling subservient to them. It assumes that the commercial negotiation is taking place between equals. An assertive style will involve asking open questions and following up with more probing questions. It treats the other person with respect and involves giving them the opportunity to make their case without interruption. This also has the benefit of allowing us to really understand their argument and identify weaknesses in it. It is important that we do not personally attack the other party or use language that irritates them and makes them disinclined to make concessions.

In some situations, we use words that have huge potential to sound patronising: "Obviously, I don't have to explain the implications of my decision". It may be obvious to us but maybe not to the other party. Sometimes the word "Obviously" is deliberately used to avoid being questioned on a difficult subject. The intention is to make the other party feel that if it is obvious, they will seem stupid if they ask questions about it. A commercial negotiator on hearing the word "obviously" used on a frequent basis might start to think "Here is an area worth exploring and questioning".

Concessions

Without concession of some sort a commercial negotiation would be unlikely to go anywhere. The key to using this technique successfully is to link concessions you make to a reciprocal concession from the other side. The ideal exchange of concessions is to concede something that is easy for you to give but valuable to the other side, in exchange for something you value that is easy for them to give you.

The key words that should always spring to your mind when concessions are being discussed are "If...then..." So, if you provide for a two-year supply of spares, then we can consider letting your people have access to our research facilities. All offers should be conditional as this gives flexibility in shaping the overall package and avoids the risk of "Painting yourself into a corner".

In making concessions it is wise to avoid what Chester Karass called "Salami negotiation" where you give away the whole sausage even though you do it a slice at a time. By being clear about your priorities and finding out theirs you can identify trade-offs and "Packages" that make good commercial sense to both parties.

Emotion

Emotion may be a dirty word in the world of commercial negotiation but there is no denying that it is a powerful influence on a lot of people. Emotion can be conveyed through our body language, such as facial expression or our posture. It can also be conveyed by our words. Sometimes we have no control over these, and we send out signals to the other party that undermines our stance. At other times if we are "Emotionally Intelligent" we can use it let the other party know how we are feeling to our advantage". As Van Kleef, De Dreu, & Manstead observed,

"Disappointment and worry, on the other hand, inform the other that one has received less than expected and signal that one is in need of compensation."

So, we can send deliberate signals about our state of mind and persuade the other party that they should be more generous or more creative. Rackham and Carlisle of Huthwaite International identified that commercial negotiators who deliberately expressed how they were feeling rather than giving away information on factual issues, were more likely to be successful.

Phrases such as "I am concerned that you do not see the potential for growth in that" or "I am delighted to see we have made progress on that scheduling issue", are useful in signalling our internal thoughts and feelings and helping the other party to see us as human rather than just as a company representative. To make use of emotion in a commercial negotiation requires self-awareness regarding our own emotions, control over which aspects of our emotions we should reveal and the ability to use emotion to motivate ourselves. This knowledge and control of our own emotions helps us to understand the emotions of others, to empathise with them and therefore communicate with them more effectively.

Power

Power or the perception of power plays a large part in any negotiation, even if no-one talks about it. Even in a principled negotiation where an explicit threat to resort to using power might seem inappropriate, it is likely that both sides will have made an assessment about what constitutes power in this commercial relationship. In many ways when the other party knows what power you have you do not need to refer to it.

We often assume that the other party has all the power in a commercial negotiation and act accordingly. Questioning the other side on how what they are proposing is better for you than going to your BATNA allows the other party to see that you have alternatives beyond doing this deal with them on the terms they are currently offering. If power is misused, although it may gain a short-term advantage, the other party will remember the feeling of being exploited and should the power shift can seek to redress the balance. Power is good to have but it is not so good if you must use it. Parties to a commercial negotiation can display their power through the words that they use or in a nonverbal way through their body language.

Framing

We would all like to think we can be persuasive, in the real world however it is easy to find that we all end up bashing our head against a metaphorical brick wall from time to time. We get the feeling that people are irrational, and research has shown that this is because generally people are quite irrational. When we present facts, we tend to do it from our perspective rather than framing them in the best terms for the other party.

A buyer in a commercial negotiation might not be keen to pay what he sees as a high price but if the solution was framed as "This will save you £5 million in 1st two years" then they might be open to persuasion. By focusing on the added value rather than the price the deal can be kept alive. Edinburgh City Council are currently considering an investment of £2bn in extending the tram system to outlying areas. Considering the trams suffered a loss of £450k in 2014 there is considerable opposition to the proposals. Professor Sean Smith of Napier Institute for Sustainable Construction agrees that people might think "Oh Jings not a lot of money on the trams again", but he is convinced that by framing negotiation round the ability to "Create places where people want to live" due to "Ushering in fresh development, jobs and cash" will make it seem a much more attractive proposition.

Many Professional Negotiators recommend the following:

- Best way to get what you want is to ask for it
- Be prepared to say no but give your reasons first
- Let the other party talk, this way you gain information and insight
- Be prepared to make concessions but get something you value in return
- You need to make decisions but not too soon
- Ask open questions, then probe for more detail and rationale
- Be prepared to disagree but keep it to the issue rather than the person
- Don't ignore their ideas, build on them
- Silence is a powerful weapon if you use it in the right way
- Be aware of nonverbal communication but do not jump to conclusions

Threat of Deadlock

Eventually when the discussion and debating has crystallised some of the differences between the parties and maybe resolved some of the easier issues, we start to reach much more contentious issues where even with the best will in the world some commercial negotiations grind to a halt. The reasons for this might be the difficulty of getting stakeholder buy in, personal differences between the negotiators, misunderstanding of a key issue or a gap that seems too big to bridge.

At this point the skilled commercial negotiator can really add value to their organisation. In order to add this value, it helps to bear in mind the reason why we are negotiating in the first place and considering the importance of both this deal and the overall relationship. A tool such as the Thomas and Killman model can help to clarify their options. It allows them to weigh up the relative importance of meeting their own needs and the importance of meeting the needs of the other party.

Knowing where this negotiation is on the quadrant can inform the negotiator on what they can do to move the situation forward. The skills that come into play at this stage of the negotiation will depend on a thorough analysis of the risks and rewards involved. None of the approaches will work in all circumstances but a flexible commercial negotiator will be able to adopt the appropriate approach to fit the scenario.

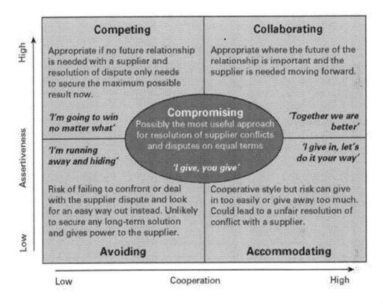

Figure 1: Threat of Deadlock

Avoid

It is a common view that to avoid discussing difficult issues is a sign of weakness and it might be in some circumstances. Taking an ostrich like approach is not going to make the issue vanish into thin air. Successful negotiators generally realise that by addressing areas of difference and difficulty and airing these that they can move on to resolve them, perhaps "Nipping these potential roadblocks in the bud".

There might be circumstances where it pays to avoid tackling an issue in the short term, perhaps because things are getting a bit emotional and it pays not to say something you might regret. Avoiding the conflict here allows for reflection and cooling off. It may be that by avoiding an issue where we lack information, we can take steps to get that information. In commercial negotiations if we avoid debate and discussion on too many areas of difference the risk is, we end up with an agreement which lacks commitment, and these resurface during implementation.

Accommodate

Phrases such as "The customer is always right" are not uncommon, particularly in a selling environment. In a commercial negotiation where the relationship overall is of more importance than a single topic or a single deal there will be times when you must say "OK, have it your way". In taking this approach commercial negotiators are gambling that they will get something of equal or greater value in return at some stage in the future.

As in any gamble there is no certainty that this will be the case. There is also the risk that if the other party gets what they want for doing nothing, them doing nothing starts to look like a great strategy to adopt. When you must or feel that it is best to do this you should ensure that you do not do so without considering your least acceptable outcome and your BATNA. Over the longer term, it would not make commercial sense to keep just giving in.

Successful commercial negotiators are much more likely to identify in advance where they can make concessions to accommodate the other party's needs and what they can ask for in return.

Compete

Commercial negotiation is sometimes perceived as a bit of a warzone anyway and some people cannot help themselves, finding that their competitive instinct kicks in and the challenge of extracting real value from the other party makes them act in a way they may not have intended. There is no doubt that in most negotiations there are issues where, if we do not get what we want the deal does not actually make good commercial sense.

In these circumstances the commercial negotiator is faced with a choice of taking a competitive stance, putting the other party's needs to one side and focusing strongly on their own. This might involve being more assertive, refusing to see any value in the other side's proposals and countering proposals with immediate counter proposals. A commercial negotiator in competitive mode will be less likely to react visibly to offers from the other side, utilising the "poker face" to avoid giving away information the other side might find useful. Accepting that in a commercial negotiation situation, this can happen and can work as some people will be intimidated by it, the risk is that the other party responds in kind and the issues get forgotten as the meeting deteriorates into a battle of wills. Even if this approach is successful in the short term, if a someone feels themselves to have competed and lost, they might try to get their own back next time. This might be a win / lose situation, but it leaves it leaves the potential for future conflict in any deal agreed.

Collaborate

The collaboration approach is one where the commercial negotiator is aiming to meet the needs of both parties. As this is aiming for a win / win outcome this would seem to be ideal. So why do we not just forget about the other approaches and just use this one?

To meet the needs of the other party and your own you need to be clear about what they are. To get this clarity involves doing significant research, building up a relationship where they are happy to disclose key information to us and are trust us to do the same in return. All of this takes time and sometimes in the commercial world this is not available. It might also be the case that this commercial negotiation does not warrant that level of investment. For those that do the parties involved should be willing to be open and honest about what their priorities are and make use of facilitation skills rather than try to dictate terms.

A collaborative approach will help get all the issues on the table so that trade-offs can be discussed, and deadlocks avoided or resolved. If the benefits of a collaborative approach are recognised, the skills of asking powerful questions, listening effectively and reading signals assume even more importance. In addition, the negotiator should be looking to build on contributions from the other side as if they can incorporate the other party's thinking into their proposals, they will maximise the chance of buy in from them. The proposal will seem like "Our idea" rather than "Their idea".

Compromise

The concept of splitting the difference or agreeing to meet in the middle is an attractive proposition to many commercial negotiators, it might seem like a sensible approach to save time or to resolve a difficult issue but at the end of the day the consequence is often two parties who are less than satisfied with the outcome of the commercial negotiation.

Given that it may not always be the ideal solution an element of compromise will often be involved in any successful negotiations, even if only until a more advantageous longer-term resolution can be found.

Agreement and Close

At some point in a commercial negotiation the parties need to agree a deal or agree that a deal is not going to happen. Sometimes this happens unexpectedly when an offer is accepted out of the blue, a more likely scenario is that the parties start to realise that they have achieved some common ground and they can see that having invested effort and energy in reaching this stage they would prefer to keep what they have than go back to scratch or whatever their BATNA situation was.

The psychology of commercial negotiators is not at this point to just accept what is on the table but to recognise that if there is something, they want that they have not introduced it better be introduced soon. In previous stages discussion might have revolved round "What might we trade?" In this stage, it is "What will we trade?" When it is apparent that the end game is near it is good practice to make use of clarifying and summarising behaviour to ensure that the parties are under no illusions about what any agreement is likely to look like. Having summarised the existing position, it is likely that the parties will propose what needs to be done for the deal to be stuck. In doing this research suggests that it is good practice to use a range and for your real target to be at the bottom of this range. "OK we can accept that, if you are prepared to give us between £781k and £884K (where £781 K is your real target) this is known as a "Bolstering range" (Ames and Mason).

The use of a range makes the offer seem more flexible but the high £884K figure "Anchors" their response at a level above our real target. The use of precise figures instead of rounded figures £800K will also give the proposal added credibility.

Psychologically it is preferable to be the party who is doing the summarising as the as this will be the default position for the agreement. The other party will need to identify any inconsistency between the summary and the discussion and point out the discrepancy. In situations where a visual aid is being used to capture the summary it is worthwhile aiming for some numerical balance between the issues so be prepared to chunk up or down as appropriate. If it is seen as fair, they are more likely to accept it. To ensure their buy in at this stage it is important to show the other party that their needs have been met and that the gap between the parties identified in the "Opening" phase has been closed to both party's satisfaction.

Be aware that at this stage the temptation to "Split the difference "will rear its head. If you hear this from the other party, you should be thinking "They have already mentally moved half way in our direction". Even if you are tempted to compromise in this way you might ask yourself, "Do I need to split 50/50 or is it reasonable to push for 70/30 in our favour"?

In this closing phase, techniques to bring the negotiation to a conclusion include referring to the opening phase and showing all issues are now settled. "We stated at the outset that we would be looking for X, Y and Z. Are we now in agreement that X, Y and Z have been achieved?". Time is also a powerful motivator to bring about a conclusion and phrases such as "We have spent six hours on this, we need to conclude before the next audit, can we do this today or do we need to come back tomorrow?". Sometimes even a simple "Have we got a deal?" is all it takes.

Recording the Agreement
Even though participants agree in the room, there is a need to record exactly what has been agreed. The output from a discussion might be the foundation for a purchase order, a contract, a project or an international trade agreement and as such must be documented. As well as being good practice and providing an audit trail, this allows the parties to use the information captured at this stage to identify how they might improve in the future. They can identify what their initial objectives were, whether they achieved them or not, if not, how close did they get and what barriers did they encounter. The detail that must be captured includes but is not limited to the obligations and responsibilities of the party's, contingencies in the event of certain circumstances, options for pursuing disputes and enforcement of contractual remedies.

They can identify lessons learnt and take steps to share that knowledge widely within their organisation. It is good practice to follow up on projected outcomes after the commercial negotiation is completed as it is important that deals do not just look good on paper but are commercially viable and deliver the outcomes that were agreed. The National Audit Office report on The BBC's management of strategic contracts identified "The BBC Trust approves strategic contracts in part based on forecast savings. It does not follow up whether forecast savings for individual strategic contracts have been delivered."

Chapter Summary
In this chapter, we considered

- The characteristics of Positional and Principled negotiation and how this might affect the psychology of commercial negotiators
- How the negotiation event itself broke down into four main stages, Opening, Discussion and Debate, Threat of Deadlock, Agreement and Close.
- The behaviours and approaches commercial negotiators might use to

persuade and influence their counterparts
- Alternative approaches to take when faced with a conflict or deadlock situation
- Recording the outcome of the Commercial negotiation

Case Study

Ahmed is a procurement manager for Zero Doubt Supplies and has just returned from a negotiation with a potential new contractor for a filtration system which is due to be rolled out across their sites in Europe, Asia and North Africa. He is reviewing his meeting with his manager, Leo.

Ahmed: "Sorry to be a pain but can I talk some things through about the meeting?"
Leo: "No problem, so, how did it go?"
Ahmed: "I feel quite frustrated actually, I am sure that looking at the figures and reviewing at the research we carried out that a deal should have been possible. At the meeting though we just seemed to go around in circles. I am not sure I am cut out for the world of commercial negotiation."
Leo: "Don't be too hard on yourself, tell me a bit more about it."
Ahmed: "Sure, here are the notes I scribbled down at the time, if you can read them, sorry my writing is not the best".

They are interrupted by Sara the CPO who needs to drag Ahmed away.

Leo: "Leave your notes with me Ahmed, they might give me some clues."

On reading the notes later Leo sees the following remarks by the contractor highlighted by Ahmed:
- "I am making you a very generous offer."
- "Obviously, I don't need to explain this to someone with your experience."
- "We are world leader in this technology, you won't get another supplier with our expertise."
- "It's not our fault your engineers do not understand these issues."
- "That's just typical, focusing on costs rather than benefits."

Task

Leo thinks he understands what the problem might have been, what do you think?

CHAPTER 8 | Reaching Agreement

Introduction

"A contract is an ask game, and if it asks for an hour, and I submit to an hour, then it's an hour. When I look at a contract, I look at the obligation - where, when, how long, the compensation. If I agree to it, that's the way it is. I have an obligation. They have an obligation." – Chuck Berry

A lot of things are said in a commercial negotiation. Some of these might be bluffs, some might be deadly serious, others a mere statement of opinion, there might even be an element of humour from time to time. The end game is however the same as it was for Chuck Berry. Not just an agreement but a legally binding contract where both parties will have rights and obligations.

In this chapter, we will look at how we turn the results of a commercial negotiation into an agreement that both parties will respect and can be enforced in law. The whole point of a commercial negotiation is to reach an agreement which will deliver added value to the participants or at least give the perception that the agreement adds value. It is important that the agreement works in the real world rather than just looks good on paper. We will consider how we can assure this by agreeing clear Key Performance Indicators (KPIs), ensuring that the terms of the agreement are not seen as punitive, preventing the risk of misrepresentation and turning the issues we have been negotiating about into a contractual agreement. We will explore some of the barriers that typically appear at this stage and suggest common sense steps to overcome these.

Reaching an agreement in discussions in a complex commercial negotiation is often just the start of a process which can last for a period of years. The agreement which people think has been reached is just the starting point for more detailed work on specific contractual terms, the ethics of the working relationship and an understanding of the roles and responsibilities of each party.

Heads of Agreement

It is important that the agreement which comes into existence in written or electronic format is an accurate representation of the discussion which has led up to it. Unethical or manipulative behaviour such as trying to "sneak" something into an agreement which has not been discussed is not only unethical and certain to damage the relationship but could give the other party the right to void the agreement. Minutes or action points recording the progress of the commercial negotiation can be turned into a "Heads of Agreement". This is a non-legally binding document which is used to record and reconcile the terms of the parties to the agreement.

The purpose of this document is to act as a guideline and is a tentative step towards a formal, fully binding contract. The content of a Heads of Agreement document will obviously vary depending on the complexity and criticality of the deal but might well include some of the following topics:

- The background to the agreement, key principles or purpose of the agreement
- Obligations of both parties
- Definitions and interpretations
- Outline pricing arrangements, liability for expenses
- Key milestones
- Commencement and expiry dates
- Dispute resolution procedures
- Confidentiality restrictions
- Information on law and jurisdiction

Contract Formation

To have an agreement which is legally binding it is necessary to be able to identify that the mandatory elements for contract formation are in place. The requirements themselves will vary depending on the jurisdiction in which the contract is being made.

In English law the "Holy trinity" of Offer, Acceptance and Consideration would need to be in place in addition to elements such as Genuineness of consent, Capacity, Legality and Intention to create legal relations. The parties need to analyse the discussions to identify clearly what offers have been made by each. To Identify what constituted an unqualified acceptance of that offer and to be clear about the consideration that will pass between them.

There have been some cases which have come to court where the traditional idea of offer and acceptance has been challenged including a 2004 case between Apple Corp Ltd and Apple Computer Inc but this was not developed in subsequent cases. The ideal contract agreed will be one which motivates the parties to work in a collaborative manner, create added value and effectively manage the risks that have been identified. The formal contract will be a synthesis of the interests and needs of both parties setting out exactly the rights and obligations of the parties. It will take account of precontractual statements made by the parties and turn these into clauses which are legally binding on them.

Pre-contractual Statements and the Risk of Misrepresentation

In concluding commercial negotiation sense must be made of several statements that will have been between the parties. These include:

Representations – Pre-contractual statements of fact made to induce the other party to enter into a contract.

Misrepresentations – False pre-contractual statements of fact made to induce the other party to enter into a contract This can be either innocent, negligent or fraudulent.

If one party makes a representation in a commercial negotiation, believing it to be true but subsequently discovers it is untrue they still have a duty to disclose this to their counterpart. If, a misrepresentation in a commercial negotiation, is discovered by the injured party they will have the right to have the contract rescinded and claim for damages. In a 2013 case "Sear v Kingfisher Buildings Ltd" damages of almost £300 000 were ordered to be paid as a result of Fraudulent Misrepresentation. When you consider the costs, time and effort expended in commercial negotiation it is wise to be cautious about making claims of fact if the cannot be substantiated. Making claims about your opinion or about your future intentions leave you on much safer ground.

It is possible in English law to attempt to limit your liability for innocent or negligent misrepresentation in your express terms of contract although to do so you must pass the tests of reasonableness of the Unfair Contract Terms Acts 1977.

Contractual Statements

Statements which are included in the contract can be classified in a number of different ways including but not limited to theses shown below:

Express terms

Probably the majority. Those terms expressly agreed between the parties, most likely to be written down.

Implied terms

Those terms not expressly agreed but incorporated into the contract through statute law or custom and practice.

Conditions
Those terms which are fundamental to the contract, breach of which gives rise to a right of termination

Warranties
Those terms which are of a less fundamental nature, breach of which gives rise to a right to claim damages.

Once terms are incorporated into the contract via the process of offer and acceptance, there may still be differences of opinion over how they should be interpreted. Although there are judicial tests that can be applied it is a good idea to make the terms as clear and as unambiguous as possible. The party who attempts to insert a term into the contract will find that in cases of dispute or ambiguity a court will place the least positive interpretation of that term in reaching their decision. This is known as the Contra Proferentum rule.

Negotiated Terms
As the parties in a commercial negotiation are human, they will no doubt fall into the same traps as anyone else. It is likely that they will want to protect themselves from risks, allocate risks between the parties in a way that seems to favour their side and focus their attention on the consequences of the other side not meeting their responsibilities.

The International Association of Contract and Commercial Management (IACCM) have identified that because of this, much time is spent on negotiating clauses such as Indemnities, liabilities and other terms where self-protection is the focus. Whilst protecting your organisation against risk might be an appropriate and practical strategy in some commercial negotiations, there might be others, where taking this narrow view prevents us from seeing the opportunities for more collaborative value creation in the terms of contract.

Where there is enough trust between the parties, the agreement might include terms which specify how reducing cycle time, lowering whole life costs and increasing revenue can be triggers for terms which arrange for both parties to share in this improvement. There might be bonus payments for exceeding the agreed Service Level Agreements (SLAs) or some other incentive mechanism which is motivational for both parties. It is likely that both parties have standard terms and conditions and in an ideal world would favour their own as they are designed to protect their interests. In a complex commercial negotiation, the terms and conditions are sometimes as important a variable as price or delivery. The mix of terms that are negotiated will vary depending on the complexity and the criticality of the agreement but as a commercial negotiator you need to understand certain fundamentals.

It is important to remember that the language you use in articulating your requirements needs to clearly spell out what you want and be specific enough to enforce in the event of a dispute, it also has to be reasonable enough for the other party to accept it. The commercial negotiator should bear in mind the following:

- Rights / Responsibility – who is responsible for what?
- Rationale – why is this term so important and why do we want it in the contract?
- Language – articulated in a clear way that allows enforcement

Common terms which need to be negotiated might include:

- Payment
- Consequential loss
- Limitation of liability
- Dispute resolution
- Termination
- Scope of work

If we use Payment terms as an example the negotiator would understand:

- Rights / responsibilities
- What gives rise to a right to payment, consequences for default, interest chargeable?
- Rationale
- The more precisely the term is defined the less likely to have fee disputes
- Language – challenge language that allows for payment without satisfactory performance, use language that will allow you to withhold payment for disputed invoices

The skilled commercial negotiator can build up their understanding of negotiated terms using this framework so that they can negotiate round most contractual terms with confidence. The language the commercial negotiator uses in contract terms is very important. Certain phrases and words such as "We will try to"; "It is our intention to…" should be avoided as they are vague, difficult to quantify and capable of being interpreted in different ways.

Stakeholder Engagement and Buy-in

It is tempting to think that at this stage the hard work is done, this is dangerous thinking. Before the agreement is finalised the skilled commercial negotiator, who is focused on the long-term success of the agreement will ensure that key stakeholders who will impact and be impacted on by the contract can review and give approval for the negotiated agreement.

Use of a tool such as RACI checklist which establishes appropriate action and communication takes place with those stakeholders.

R Responsible
A Accountable
C Consulted
I Informed

Typical stakeholder involvement might include:

- Finance, they will be concerned that budget is available, what contingent liabilities might emerge and impact on cashflow.
- Legal teams may be involved from the start or may just need to review the final agreement to ensure, the agreement is one which will be legally binding and to be clear about the risks involved.
- HR, what impact will the contract have on our people? What are the health and safety implications?

Key Performance Indicators (KPIs)

KPIs are used by contracting parties to evaluate the standard of delivery of a range of contractual activities. The focus can be on consistency, excellence, speed or cost but in any event, it is important that commercial negotiators have a solid understanding of key activities from the point of view of their organisation.

This point of view needs to be reflected in the KPIs embedded into the contract. In some cases, it might be possible to negotiate KPIs into a contract after it has been placed but by doing it prior to contract award you maximise the chances that the other party will buy into them as opposed to feeling they have been imposed retrospectively.

Identify What to Measure?

The list could be exhaustive, so to ensure that relevant KPIs are utilised the organisation could make use of a balanced Scorecard method which originated from Dr Robert Kaplan in Harvard Business school in the early 1990's. It is possible to use the score card merely to measure operational performance, although it is more effective when utilised in a more strategically focused manner. It is vital that they show the whole picture not just a small part of it. Typical perspectives to focus on might include:

- Financial measures
- Customer / stakeholder measures
- Internal business processes
- Learning and development

Developing an effective system

- Identifying the critical success factors
- Determining how to measure each area
- Ensure you are driving the correct behaviour
- Obtaining buy in of internal and external stakeholders
- Monitoring for continuous improvement

Communicate results in a way that motivates?

- One of the most popular ways to display KPIs and to communicate performance results is via a KPI dashboard. The dashboard is a colourful, visual method of displaying key metrics and performance results in a way that can be easily understood.
- DPSS consultants makes use of a "Key Statements "approach to KPIs. This allows for clear definition of the standard required and achieved using a five-point scale. It is most effective if several key stakeholders are involved in the standard setting and evaluation process. More detail can be found in "Practical Procurement 2ed" by Carter et al
- Ensure successful performance of the negotiated agreement?
- Agree targets that are realistic and within the capabilities of the party responsible for the activity.
- Ensure that the agreement motivates the supplier to dedicate appropriate number and levels of resources to the activity.
- Check the other party understands their responsibilities and appreciates

they will be monitored in how they deliver to the appropriate standard.
- Create a climate where the other party shares your vision and is willing to give constructive feedback

There are many traps to be wary of regarding KPIs including, making them seem like a punishment, being unrealistic and drowning the team in unnecessary detail. An old joke suggests that it is easy to put together a seven-day weather forecast…it just takes fourteen days to do it. KPIs need to add value rather than just add work. Including KPIs as an upfront item in a commercial negotiation rather than trying to bolt them on as an afterthought is much more likely to lead to successful outcomes.

"A strategy without metrics is just a wish. And metrics that are not aligned with strategic objectives are a waste of time." – Emery Powell

Chapter Summary

In this chapter we have considered:

- Ways to turn the results of a commercial negotiation into an agreement that both parties will respect and can be enforced in law.
- We looked at how Heads of agreement can be used as a non- legally binding step on the way to agree a more fully detailed formal contract.
- The main elements needed for formation of a valid contract were outlined.
- The risk of Misrepresentation was explained with definitions of the different types and how they might occur in commercial negotiations.
- We classified the different types of contract term, identifying some of the terms which are most commonly negotiated between contracting parties to achieve the appropriate balance between risk and reward.
- The importance of achieving buy in from key stakeholders prior to ratification of the negotiated agreement was emphasised.
- The importance of and development of KPIs was described and guidance given for their successful implementation.
- We looked at the benefits of a good ethical working relationship in terms of ensuring the negotiated agreement worked in the practical real world rather than just in theory.

Case Study

Padma works as an account manager for the Celestial group who are a major international hotel chain. He has been working closely with a new client, Polar airlines who are a small but rapidly expanding airline, based in Scandinavia. His main point of contact with Polar is Karina, who has recently taken on a Category Management role within the airline.

Karina is full of ideas and is keen to explore some new ways of working with the Celestial group. She has recently attended a seminar where the benefits of Risk / Reward contracts were explained.

She is still a bit hazy on the concept but can see no reason why she should not be the first person in her company to put the theory into practice. She anticipates she will be rewarded with serious kudos if she pulls it off. She believes some of Celestials KPIs are driving the wrong behaviour and cites the contact centre who take the bookings as an example. Her research shows that customers feel they are rushed due to a KPI-focused on average handing time. She feels total time to resolution would be a more appropriate measure of effectiveness.

Although she is new to dealing with the hotel industry, she feels that the negotiations with Padma have been going well and they have managed to identify some areas where there is common ground between them and have managed to cobble together a Heads of Agreement document though there is still much to discuss.

Padma is an experienced negotiator although he is very risk averse. He knows the Celestial group are going through a difficult patch now and is aware that there are a number of internal, political and communication issues which are making his job very difficult. He is reluctant to commit Celestial to some of the KPIs that Karina is proposing as he can foresee compliance difficulties. Padma can however see the attraction of sharing some of the benefits highlighted by Karina.

Task

Advise Padma and Karina on practical steps they might take to resolve the issue. What terms might both seek to incorporate into the contract?

CHAPTER 9 | INTERNATIONAL CONTRACT AND COMMERCIAL NEGOTIATIONS

Definition

In chapter 1 we defined negotiations as a process whereby two or more commercial parties attempt to persuade each other to accept the merits of their relative bargaining and positions and to influence each other to reconcile their often-competing needs. Our definition of international contractual and commercial negotiations is essentially the same. However, the international context can increase the risk of suboptimal and unsustainable agreements is dramatically increased.

Therefore, the discipline of professional commercial negotiations, including clear aims and objectives, thorough preparation and robust negotiation strategies is even more critical. As with domestic negotiations, the negotiator's power and influence is enhanced by information about the market and the contractor, this is further enhanced by a good negotiating relationship, backed up with a sound and robust BATNA.

The Five Ps of Effective Negotiations

Our simple checklist in chapter 1 that defined the requirements for an effective negotiated outcome framed around the Five Ps is even more valid in the context of international negotiations. The international context means that:

- **Planning** for the negotiations, including aims objectives strategies and tactics. The cultural and environmental factors can greatly affect the planning process
- **Prepare** for the negotiations, including market conditions, relative bargaining positions, SWOT and participant profiles, here issues such a language, customs and traditions can greatly affect the success of international negotiations and need to be carefully researched and factored into the process
- **Participate** in the negotiations, including influencing and persuading skills, again these will be especially influenced by language, religion and customs
- **Perform** in the negotiations and achieve the aims and objectives, achieving stated goals and objectives in the international negotiation's context is even

more challenging than the local or domestic market place.

- **Postnegotiation** analysis including the benefits gained and the impact upon the relationship with the supplier

Preparation for International Negotiations

IACCM have identified seven key areas that need to be researched and understood when embarking on international negotiations. Each of which has the potential to derail commercial negotiations and each of these must be considered when preparing to enter international negotiations.

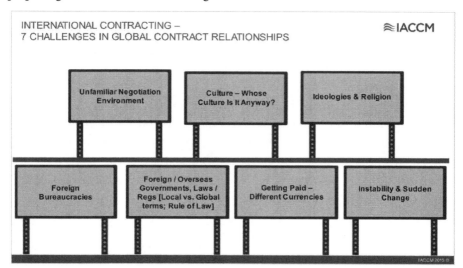

Understanding Cultural Differences

Understanding national cultural differences is more important than ever in an age of globalised supply markets and the number of cross-cultural interactions rapidly increases. For example, China's economy is already the second largest in the world and provides many industrial products and projects to the rest of the world.

The rise of Asian economies and its contractors makes it necessary for Western companies to understand how to negotiate in an Asian context. Contract and commercial managers and procurement professionals who work in global corporations need to interact with people from other cultures daily.

The West and Others

USA and European states stand out from the rest of the world for their sense of themselves as individuals. They think of themselves as unique, autonomous, self-motivated, self-made.

People in the rest of the world are more likely to see themselves as interwoven with other people as interdependent, not independent. In such social worlds, the goal is to fit in and adjust to others, not to stand out. These people imagine themselves as part of a larger whole, threads in a web, not lone horsemen on the frontier. In America, they say that the squeaky wheel gets the grease. In Japan, people say that the nail that stands up most gets hammered down.

Wheat v Rice?

Some authors believe different orientations to the social worlds are created by wheat farming and rice farming. Rice is a finicky crop, rice paddies need standing water, they require complex irrigation systems that must be built and drained each year. One farmer's water use affects his neighbour's yield. A community of rice farmers needs to work together in tightly integrated ways.

Wheat needs only rainfall, not irrigation. To plant and harvest it takes half as much work as rice does, and substantially less coordination and cooperation. Historically, Europeans and the USA have been wheat farmers, whereas Asians have grown rice. The authors of these studies argue that over thousands of years, rice and wheat-growing societies developed distinctive cultures: "You do not need to farm rice or wheat yourself to inherit associated culture."

The Context

People in the west are more likely to ignore the context and others to attend to it. A group of Americans and Japanese were shown an image of a large fish swimming among other fish and seaweed fronds. The Americans remember the single central fish first. The Japanese viewers recalled the background. They'll also remember more about the seaweed and other objects in the scene.

Cultural Dimensions

The Hofstede Model

Geert Hofstede defines culture as "The collective programming of the mind that distinguishes the members of one group or category of people from others".

Hofstede's cultural dimensions theory is a framework for cross-cultural communication. It describes the effects of a society's culture on the values of its members, and how these values relate to behaviour, using a structure derived from factor analysis. These include:

- Power Distance: the distance between individuals at different levels of a hierarchy

- Uncertainty Avoidance: more or less need to avoid uncertainty about the future
- Individualism versus Collectivism: the relations between the individual and his/her fellows
- Masculinity versus Femininity: "Tough v Tender"
- Long Term Orientation v Short Term normative – how society deals with challenges, low scores = time honoured traditions, whereas high scores = more pragmatic
- Indulgence stands for a society that allows relatively free gratification of basic and natural human drives related to enjoying life. Restraint stands for a society that suppresses gratification of needs and regulates it by means of strict social norms.

Trompenaars' Model of National Culture Differences

Another well respected model is that provided by Fons Trompenaars' model of seven national culture differences. It is a cross-cultural communication model applied to general business and management, developed by Trompenaars and Charles Hampden-Turner. This involved a large-scale survey of 8 841 managers and organization employees from 43 countries. The frame looks at different cultures by contrasting the following:

1. Rules or relationships?
2. Group or individual level?
3. Neutral vs emotional?
4. How separate are our private and work lives?
5. Status by achievement earned or given to us?
6. Perform actions one at time or a few things at same time?
7. Do we control the environment, or does it control us?

Negotiating with Rule and Relationships Cultures

Rule orientated cultures include the U.S.A, Canada, the UK, the Netherlands, Germany, Scandinavia, New Zealand, Australia and Switzerland.

Although the UK is regarded as a European "Rule" state, there are still many cultural nuances when negotiating with other European countries. In Italy, business meetings and negotiations tend to start late but parties are expected to arrive on time. In France they allow a 10-minute grace period, but it will make a good first impression in the negotiation process if you are the first person to arrive. In the United Kingdom we endeavour try to arrive at the meeting a few minutes before the scheduled start time.

Greetings and Opening the Negotiations

Handshakes are standard business greetings throughout Europe and are exchanged before and after every negotiation meeting. Maintaining eye contact and a firm handshake is customary between men, but a gentler one is often used with women.

In Italy and France, men may kiss female business associates on the cheek, but this is only if they are familiar with one another and this is much less likely to happen in the UK. When dealing with most Europeans in the negotiation context, we should always use a person's title and avoid addressing them by their first name until invited to do so. Europeans do not present business cards with both hands or consider exchanging cards as an important ritual.

Communication

To our great advantage, English is spoken in most European countries, and if you're negotiating with a young professional, then their English will likely be to a high standard. Knowing a few greetings in the language of the person you're negotiating with will make a favourable impression.

Dining and entertainment

Europeans do not usually conduct negotiations over breakfast, whereas being invited to lunch or dinner is common. Negotiating during lunch is the norm in most European countries, however in Italy, Greece or the Czech Republic they tend not discuss business unless their host initiates the conversation. Wine is normally served with meals across Europe and it is offensive to refuse, but moderation is expected.

A dinner invitation is a sign of esteem in Europe and it's considered impolite to refuse. Business talk is usually avoided during dinner but may be broached towards the end of the meal, often while dessert and/or coffee is being served.

Gifts

Apart from the UK, bringing the host a small gift is appropriate if you're invited to someone's home for dinner. If you are dining at the home of someone in the Netherlands, France or Belgium, bringing a bottle of wine can be considered offensive as it implies your host has a deficient wine cellar.

Negotiating with Relationship Cultures

Relationships cultures include Russia, Latin-America, and China. In these cultures, Professor Benoliel states, "I was struck by how important building relationships is. Whether you are negotiating in Thailand or Singapore or China, you will clearly see that people invest a great deal in building relationships and trust."

He goes on to say, "The unspoken emphasis on harmony plays out in the language used during negotiations, with Asian negotiators preferring a more subtle and metaphoric tone compared to the direct and unambiguous choice of words favoured by Western negotiators.

"The Chinese say: 'Only the devil goes straight', meaning that we should always be careful to protect the 'face' of the other person. Because of this, we should be more considerate and suggestive during negotiations rather than brutally direct,"

The preference for the indirect in Asia also extends beyond language to non-verbal communication, according to Professor Benoliel who gives the example of how eye contact is an indication of trustworthiness in the European context, however, he points out that looking people straight in the eye can be perceived as an act of aggression in Asia.

Negotiators from some more western cultures such as the UK often have difficulty adjusting to hierarchies in Asia as their workplaces tend to be more egalitarian. Japan is very hierarchical and formal and characterized by titles. If one were to greet the most junior person in the room first as opposed to the most senior person, this would cause a great deal of offence and get the negotiation off to a poor start.

Negotiating in China

China business expert and cross-cultural consultant Dr Mona Chung says there is a world of difference between Chinese and more western cultures. She states, "Everyone thinks China is a free economy now, it's not," she says. "It's a centrally planned economy." One of the big differences, Chung says, is in the communication styles and culture. For example, Australian culture and communication is low context while China is the complete opposite.

One of the most common mistakes is to assume an offer in the negotiation will be accepted when saying no is not part of the culture where the agreement is taking place. "Culturally, it's very rude and very blunt to say 'no' in China or Japan," Chung says. "When you come from a culture and language that's not vague, you are disadvantaged to start. The same word can mean different things."

Many Asian businesses, particularly in China, are built on relationships. Another mistake is focussing on the price and not the relationship in the negotiation. Europeans often think negotiating with the Chinese is always about price. That is not always the case. The Chinese would do business with people and lose money if they have to do something like keep the relationship and save face.

Communication

English is the language of business – this is major advantage for negotiators from the UK and the USA.

Many international negotiators have an excellent grasp of English, but the language is riddled with idioms and grammatical exceptions that non-native speakers often find hard to decode.

Language and Culture Issues

Marketing and sales people have always been conscious of the risks of the incorrect use of language. The brand name that conjures images of quality and reliability in one language may have serious negative connotations in another. For example, an Iranian razor manufacturer used the brand name "Tiz," the Persian word for "sharp," to illustrate the quality of its product. When the company began exporting the razors to nearby Qatar, they learned that "tiz" was the Arabic slang word for "buttocks"...

One of the most sensitive issues in any culture is its religion. The misuse of religious iconography can damage a company's image with those customers. During the 1994 World Cup, bottles of Heineken beer displayed the flags of all the participants in the tournament, including Saudi Arabia. The country's flag shows a verse from the Quran, Islam's holy book. The Quran forbids the use of alcohol, so thousands of Muslims registered complaints with the brewer for displaying the verse.

Maya Hu-Chan, leadership expert and executive coach, states that the key to effective communication lies in adapting communication styles to fit the audience. International negotiators need to consider the following when negotiating with someone for whom English is their second language:

1. Communication is always the responsibility of the communicator. It's our job to make sure your listener understands you, not the other way around.
2. Use the simplest possible words. Mark Twain once told an editor, "I never write metropolis for seven cents because I can get the same price for city. I never write policeman because I can get the same money for cop."
3. Shorter, simpler words are better – especially when communicating with a global audience.
4. Speak slowly, we don't have to enunciate every syllable but slow down when using key words or phrases and make it clear when you are switching to a new topic.
5. Ask open-ended questions instead of yes-no questions. Questions that start with who, what, where, when, why or how require longer, more thoughtful

answers, which reduces miscommunication in the long run.

6. Make the other side feel comfortable, then they will ask questions and admit when they don't understand something

Low and High Context

Low context, as is practised in the US, as "saying exactly what you mean". High context, which is common in Japan, "is leaving much to be appreciated depending on the circumstances, recognising that the world is complex, and circumstances change".

British and American English Vocabulary Differences

Although the UK and the USA are both English speaking countries, there are still many common words that do not have common meaning and different words to describe the same thing. This can cause confusion and even offence in some instances. It would not be polite to ask an American lady if she has a rubber, for example...

Chapter Summary

In this chapter we have considered:

- The nature and challenges of international negotiations
- The Five Ps of negotiation in the context of international negotiations
- The cultural dimensions of international negotiations including the Hofstede and Trompenaars' Models of cultural analysis
- The differences between negotiating with "rule" and "relationship" orientated cultures and states
- The impact of language difference in the context of international negotiations

---

Case Study – Cultural Misfits

Construction Service Consultants are a UK based company, specialising in providing onsite technical support and advise on how to improve efficiency in the context of construction operations. The company is very well respected in the market place and several of its more senior consultants are well known experts in the field, one has published a well know book entitled "Construction Improvements" everyone in the industry has a copy.

The company is contracted by the International Construction Company (ICC) based in the UAE, to provide onsite support and advice. The contract has been awarded on a fixed day rate basis and bonus, plus economy air travel. The consultants are used to travelling business class and the fare difference is quite small, but ICC has insisted. Shortly after the contract had been awarded the team of consultants arrives on site to commence the work in the Middle East, where ICC has several major operations.

An inaugural meeting with Ali, the contract administrator, which is scheduled for 10am on the first day. Ali is delayed and does not arrive until 11.30. During the meeting with the consultants Ali makes it clear that he expects the team to meet their "contractual obligations" and that he will be monitoring their progress very closely. He also implies that his own team could have undertaken this work but are too busy on more important work.

During the meeting, Ali is constantly answering calls on his mobile, many of which appear to be relating to trivial matters. Ali is keen for the improvements to benefit the local community; the consultants are more interested in achieving their targets to secure the bonus. The consultants refer to the rules of engagement, whereas Ali wants to focus on the relationship.

The consultancy team was meant to be headed up by Peter Jones, but he decided that he was too busy and has sent Ms Claudia Jordan in his place. At the meeting Claudia states that from her study of the results of previous studies, many mistakes have been made by Ali and his team (who are present at the meeting) and that his poor leadership is a key issue. She states that she will be able to show them how to do much better in the future. She also points out that some contracts seem to have been award to less than competent local contractors, at higher prices.

The consultants commence work the next day, but within a few weeks the project has come to complete stop. The consultants are complaining about a complete lack of cooperation from Ali and his team, while Ali sites arrogance on the part of the consultants. Both sides are threatening to take legal action.

Task

What has caused this relationship to breakdown and how can we get back on track?

CHAPTER 10 | EVALUATION AND LESSONS LEARNED

Introduction

"We cannot solve our problems with the same thinking that caused them." – Albert Einstein

In commercial negotiation, as in life according to Einstein, we need to be prepared to analyse what we have done, weigh up the pros and cons of those actions and decide what we can do better next time. In this chapter, we will look at how we can evaluate the success of our commercial negotiation performance, why that evaluation is so important and how we can incorporate the lessons learned into planning for the next time. We will outline a simple three step process to facilitate this learning and we will look at how this evaluation can be carried out on several different levels.

In a Negotiation training course, we can role play several negotiation scenarios to see what works, how it works and what reaction it provokes. At the end of the session we can talk about the outcomes and we can even ask the other party "What could you have given us?".

We can consider not only the financial and commercial aspects of the negotiation but also the feelings and emotions which emerged during the process and how they might influence the success of the negotiated agreement as well as the ongoing relationship.

Unfortunately, in the real world we can rarely expect such candour from our counterpart and therefore must be a bit more creative to carry out any practical assessment of our performance.

Plan, Do, Review

Plan, Do, Review is a well-established three step process which should be easy to grasp. In real life, unfortunately some people habitually slip into a cycle of Plan, Do, Plan, Do, Plan, Do. They only review how things have gone when a disaster strikes. In commercial negotiation to fall into this trap is to miss out on significant opportunities to add value to your organisation. If we achieve a great result in a commercial negotiation how crazy would it be not to share the secret and to ensure that it can be recognised, remembered and repeated.

In earlier chapters, we identified the type of planning we needed to do, the information we should gather, how we set objectives and planned how we would achieve these

We looked at how we would carry out the commercial negotiation, implement our strategy, make use of the skills within the team and discussed tactics to use throughout the different phases of the negotiation attempting to gain a win / win agreement. We looked at how to negotiate round key variables and exchange concessions which were valuable to us for concessions which were easy for us to give.

At the Review stage, we now need to consider how well we did in each of the previous stages, identify areas for improvement in process, personal approach and tactics. We need to get feedback from stakeholders on how well their needs have been met and we probably need to carry out the review not just immediately after the deal has been done but after a longer time period has elapsed to assess how well longer-term benefits have been accrued.

By carrying out this evaluation the commercial negotiator not only satisfies him or herself that they have done a good job but also contributes to good practice and continuous improvements in areas such as:

- Avoiding legal issues
- Identifying areas of good practice
- Identify where mistakes have been made and take appropriate corrective action
- Taking steps to improve long term relationships
- Contribution to cost reduction and process improvement
- Improvement of knowledge management strategy
- Formative and Summative Evaluation

Formative evaluation is an internal method of judging the worth of an activity while it is in progress. This part of the evaluation focuses on the process we have gone through to achieve the results we have.

Summative evaluation is a more external way to judge the value of an activity at its conclusion or summation. The focus is on the outcome.

"When the cook tastes the soup, that's formative; when the guests taste the soup, that's summative." – Robert Stakes

A commercial negotiator will be likely to carry out formative evaluations at a number of different stages in the negotiation process. This might be in confirming that key stakeholders buy into objectives prior to carrying out the commercial negotiation, checking that the negotiation team has the appropriate balance of skills and assessing the strengths, weaknesses, opportunities and threats for both sides. Once the commercial negotiation has been concluded, it is good practice to review how successful it has been. Since generally the commercial negotiator is not working on their own account but for stakeholders, it is important to involve them in this evaluation in the long run. In the short term, however it is also important to gauge the initial reaction as soon after conclusion as possible.

Questions such as "How did that go?" "Did we get a good deal? "How close to our most desirable outcome did we get?" will give us a feeling about the success of the negotiation. Whilst normally used to gauge the impact of training programmes, we might find the Kirkpatrick evaluation framework as a useful model to help us structure this process of trying to identify the lessons learned post commercial negotiation.

Reaction

As discussed above, we usually want to carry out an initial review to assess "How well did we do?" "Did we achieve our objectives?" Did we feel good about our performance or not?

Learning

What new information did we gain through that process? How might that information be used in future commercial negotiations? How might we refine our processes? What extra training will benefit our commercial negotiators? What did we learn about the other party?

Behaviour

Whilst evaluation of reaction and learning, will take place as soon as possible, the evaluation of the behavioural level can only take place after the commercial negotiator has a chance to put some of the learned behaviour into practice. The organisation and individuals can now start to assess if the learning has resulted in more appropriate negotiating behaviour throughout the organisation.

If there has been no improvement, what barriers have still to be overcome? At this stage, as the implementation of the commercial agreement has begun there should also be a wealth of information which was mere supposition at an earlier stage. Discussions can take place involving both procurement and supplier personnel to evaluate and provide feedback to each other on key aspects of the agreement.

Results

The ultimate success of organisational learning is measured by whether the learning is translated into more effective behaviour which generates improved results. Evaluation at this level is the most difficult to carry out as it is not always easy to isolate improvements in results down to specific improved behaviours and it is also difficult to attribute even these behaviours to learning from a specific commercial negotiation or negotiations.

It is likely that for this evaluation to add any value it should involve key stakeholders at a senior level within the organisation. As Bill Gates commented, "Your most unhappy customers are your greatest source of learning". So questions like 'What aspects of the commercial negotiation are key stakeholders happy or unhappy with?', or 'Did the negotiation deliver the results that the stakeholders were promised at the planning stage?' are all critical to the learning process. What feedback can the senior stakeholders provide about how well their needs have been met? What impact has the negotiation had on Key Performance Indicators (KPIs)?

Single and Double Loop Learning

One problem that frequently emerges from commercial negotiations is that when we ask ourselves how did we do? We want to reassure ourselves that we have done a good job and added value to the organisation. We want to avoid the cognitive dissonance that comes from finding out that, the deal we have struck will be one that does not yield the expected profit or will be very difficult to enforce as we have been a bit too generous or a bit too rigorous. Our initial analysis of "How did we do?" even when we find out things we could have done better, tends to focus on corrective actions for these things. This is an example of single loop learning as identified by Argyris.

In single loop learning the emphasis is on the tools and techniques we have utilised, and we consider how we used them or if there are other techniques that would be more useful. There is a place for this type of evaluation and getting it right will allow our organisation to carry on doing business in a steady state environment and achieve its current objectives. We make use of the information we have obtained through the process of commercial negotiation to improve the way we do what we do.

Given the complex, longer term issues that can be encompassed in today's commercial negotiations there is frequently a need to look beyond the way we do things now and to challenge some more fundamental aspects of our business. This double loop learning, rather than questioning, "Was that an effective question?" would focus on "What assumptions were we making when we asked that question?". By focusing our analysis on this deeper level, we can uncover more basic truths regarding the strategic direction of the company. By asking ourselves.

- "Why was that important?"
- "How does this impact the way we do business?"
- "Was our BATNA completely unrealistic then?"
- "Should we really do business with companies like that?"

We can build our understanding of our own drivers and those of our counterparts. Without looking at the rationale for our actions we risk operating in a vacuum and constantly treating symptoms of a problem rather than the cause. Over time we will learn to recognise and label a range of strategies and behaviours that work well for us. These are the things we want to build on and make the most of. We will also understand that some tactics and ploys do not come naturally to us. These aspects can be developed so that though they may not be our first choice, we can deploy them if they are the only option.

To ensure we are getting the most for our evaluation, we should avoid the "Blunderbuss" approach where we try to blast everything. It makes sense to focus on the key areas for the organisation and evaluate how the learning from the commercial negotiation impacts on these. It is likely that as an organisation we have some form of Balanced scorecard as discussed in Chapter 8. Depending on the organisation, the industry and the environment, the headings may vary but could be like the four used below. This balanced scorecard can be used to structure our approach to the evaluation of our commercial negotiations.

Balanced Scorecard approach

- Strategic
- What happened in the commercial negotiation that impacts on the organisations ability to fulfil its Vision / Mission statements?
- Financial
- How will the negotiated agreement contribute to the bottom line? What are the problems we now see in enforcing financial terms which were not apparent before?
- Operational
- What are the challenges faced in implementing this in a practical way for operational purposes?
- Relationship
- What impact has the commercial negotiation had on the relationship between the parties involved. What potential is there for working more closely in the future as a result of this deal? Which party is in a stronger position after conclusion of this agreement?

Importance of Lessons Learned

The nature of the relationship will affect the nature of the evaluation which takes place. Some cases may not necessitate as much in-depth analysis as others. The resources dedicated to the evaluation will relate to the potential benefits expected to be realised and the level of risk involved. Sometimes the evaluation might be carried out by both sides independently of each other. In cases where the commercial negotiation leads to an ongoing relationship where both parties have a lot at stake, the case needs to be made for joint evaluation with key stakeholders from each side. This evaluation workshop might benefit from the use of a trained facilitator to provide focus and to keep things objective and ensure that a genuine two-way exchange of learning takes place. The benefits of working in this way include:

- Demonstrates commitment to continuous improvements
- Secures involvement of key stakeholders
- Provides a forum for honest objective feedback
- Gets contentious issues out in the open and work towards resolution
- Ask "What if...?" questions of each party
- Builds trust
- Failure to Learn Lessons
- Missing out on potential innovation
- Remain rooted to outmoded ideas
- Relationships enter a destructive spiral
- Knowledge Management

If, as Francis Bacon claimed in 1597, 'Knowledge is Power', surely it is a wise choice not only to get as much knowledge as possible but to understand what leverage having that Knowledge gives us. Bill Gates once claimed that most of the value of his organisation lay not in software or hardware but in "walking around in the heads of the employees." The value of the things which people have learned including the things they have learned from participating in commercial negotiations is sometimes known as "tacit knowledge" (Michael Polanyi).

Sometimes, people can do things very effectively but not know how or why. Successful knowledge management programmes strive to turn this knowledge into "codified or explicit knowledge". So that the knowledge is retained in procedures, processes and practices.

This process will involve various stages, typically:

- Capture
- Analysis

- Specification
- Capture

Capturing the information will need a combination of good note-taking skills and the ability to remember key information. I remember a colleague telling me "We all have a photographic memory...but not all are developed". What did I do? What did they do? What was the outcome? How did I feel?

Analysis
Having captured relevant information, the negotiation team should analyse it to assess the potential impact on relationships, future strategy, commercial negotiation training, planning systems etc. Where was there evidence of duplication of effort? What information did I need that I did not have? How could we have got access to that information? This level of analysis benefits from personal interaction as "Bouncing ideas off one another" allows for the information to be looked at from a variety of angles and the participants are able to build on the ideas of others.

Specification
It is important that the learning from commercial negotiation is capable of being used throughout the organisation. Findings from the analysis phase need to be simplified and turned into documents, processes and procedures that allow us to improve future communications, give clear guidance for future commercial negotiations and facilitates a move to a more effective commercial negotiation culture.

Chapter Summary
In this chapter we considered:

- How we could evaluate the success of a commercial negotiation using a Plan, Do, Review process
- We identified a number of levels on which we could evaluate this success, looking at Reaction, Learning, Behaviour and Results
- We explored the importance of taking on board the learning from commercial negotiation and the consequences of failing to do so
- The importance of the involvement of key stakeholders in the evaluation process was explained
- The characteristics of formative and summative evaluation and single and double loop learning were described

- We looked at how the learning from commercial negotiations could benefit the organisations knowledge management strategy

---

Case Study

Shirley is a business Partner at Venga Plc who specialise in Corporate Services Outsourcing and she has spent the last year putting together an agreement with Energos Plc throughout their European and North African operations. Both companies have high hopes for high levels of synergy from this Strategic Alliance and have thrown a huge amount of resource at it to make sure it delivers benefits for both parties. Juan is the Chief Procurement Officer for Energos and has had the closest dealings with Shirley in negotiating the terms of the agreement.

Angela is a senior manager in the Operations Division of Energos and is concerned that her counterparts at Venga seem to be unclear regarding their responsibilities and she is constantly besieged by junior people asking her for things she can see as "Nice to have" but not really in line with the organisation's strategic priorities. She finds that Shirley is always coming up with suggestions which although they might save some money, seem to conflict with the Energos people values. Angela is sure that Juan would have spelled out these people values during the commercial negotiation.

Juan has found working with Shirley quite stressful and finds it difficult to get her to admit to difficulties in the implementation of the agreement. He is keen to introduce an improved system for measuring customer satisfaction. With the service provided by would like to work with them to agree an appropriate way to do this. The current system is based o a form where the customer is given the opportunity to rate the service as Excellent, Good, Poor or Very Poor. Angela's management team have expressed concerns to Juan as to the accuracy of this method of working and state that "The scores do not match the comments".

Shirley prides herself on her creativity and appreciation of the big picture and finds Juan with his attention to detail frequently has her on her back foot. At the most recent review meeting Juanwas constantly digging down into the statistics regarding a number of issues and the cost implications of these. Shirley has recently identified that due to mistakes in Energos provided information, they were paying for services they did not receive and others which they received were not paid for. The cost benefit from this discovery was in favour of Energos but she felt that Juan gave Venga no credit for this. Shirley can see many opportunities for

---

improving operations, but Juan seems more concerned with "tiptoeing" round his internal stakeholders, contrary to the impression he gave during the negotiations.

Task

- What learning opportunities exist for both companies?
- How can they use this learning for their mutual benefit?

CHAPTER 11 | CONTRACT MANAGEMENT AND NEGOTIATION – POST AWARD

Introduction

The contract when signed should not be viewed as a sacred text that cannot be changed. If the contract is not working, or if there is reason to believe it will not deliver the desired outcomes, then we need to be proactive in identifying and negotiating necessary changes.

Contract Execution

Once the negotiation has been completed then the successful and unsuccessful contractors must be notified, and the contract signed and executed. In most cases the contract signatory will be the client divisional manager (or equivalent) and the contractor's representative will then sign and return. Copies of the executed contract will be sent to the contract manager, contracting section and finance to facilitate payments and financial control. Notification of the decision to both successful and unsuccessful bidders will be the responsibility of contracting section.

Although the sales side of the commercial negotiation has been completed, that may not be the end of the negotiation process. This is especially true in the case of strategic services and bottleneck contracts. As these contracts are implemented and roll out, there are likely to be many opportunities for post award negotiation. These could include contractual variations, revised KPIs and SLAs, changes to contract scope and outcomes.

Transition to Contract Managers

The seamless transfer and implementation of the negotiated agreement to the designated contract manager(s) is a vital part of the process. In many instances, the contract manager will have been involved in the sourcing process. The handover team will have a series of aims and objectives, these will include:

- To generate the foundations for the contract delivery
- Generate a comprehensive handover plan
- Inform all key stakeholders that the contract is to commence
- Set up contract tracking systems
- Commence reporting process to senior stakeholders

- Undertake risk assessment and develop mitigation strategies
- Engage with all key stakeholders
- Nominate designated contract manager & delivery team
- Set up all contract logs and databases
- The outcomes for these actions will include:
- Board reporting documentation
- Stakeholder dialogue set-up
- Updated risk register
- Updated contracts register
- Robust Handover plan
- Record in Supplier Database
- File signed contract securely

Managing the Handover Process

There are many factors that must be understood and addressed to ensure a seamless transfer for procurement to contract management, these include:

Understand the Negotiation Background

The contract manager needs to fully appreciate the background to the signed contract. This will include the original Contract Mandate, and issues addressed during the commercial negotiations. These will include the transition of the risk, quality, HSE, and other log documents compiled during the commercial negotiation phase. Reference to the negotiating plan and strategy will be required and will help understand the activities leading up to contract signature. It maybe that at win/lose outcome could have a negative impact on the rolling out of the contract. A detailed Handover Plan or checklist should be used to manage this area, along with engagement with the key stakeholders. Frequent reference to the quality, time and cost metrics negotiated regarding contract performance will be required with associated plans agreed with the supplier to ensure delivery to plan are required at this stage.

Ensure Access to Resources

The contract manager will need to identify and negotiate for the resources and personnel required and those of the supplier. These are contained within the contract plan, and effectively managed within the budget. Engagement with key stakeholders is vital and records regarding any internal commercial negotiations should be maintained through the contract logs. Within each contract, a different set of personnel resources and roles may need to be negotiated. Careful analysis of these is required to ensure the optimum return from the contract activity, and to add optimum value from the contract activity. Principled commercial negotiations with the supplier may enable closer working relationships and sharing of information to improve this efficiency.

Undertake Risk Management

In every contract, there is some element of risk. The contract parties need to have a clear and coordinated view on what risks are present and ensure that these are logged using the Risk Log, and an effective and aligned risk management process has been undertaken within the contract activity and on an ongoing basis to understand and manage the risks. These risks will typically fall into one of four categories: Treated, Tolerated, Transferred or Terminated but a unified and principled commercial negotiation approach by the parties will improve resilience and improve efficiency.

Engaging and Negotiating with Stakeholders

It is critical that there is a common understanding the requirements of supplier and the contractor manager as well as both primary and secondary stakeholders. This is essential to understand the quality, time, and cost demands from the contract. Each of these core contract metrics should be negotiated, logged, and referenced within the contract plan and ongoing contract activity.

London Heathrow Terminal 5

A classic example of poor handover is that of BA and Terminal 5. The construction of T5 was heralded as textbook case of a successful project, delivered on time and to cost. However, when it came to open the new terminal, the transition was a failure.

The BBC reported that despite months of preparations at T5, its problems began almost immediately as staff arrived for their morning shifts. Many British Airways airport workers complained they were delayed getting to the building because of a shortage of specially-designated car parking spaces. Some also reported that staff overflow car parks were not open, and they had been forced to drive around in circles to find somewhere to put their cars. Then, once inside the terminal building, workers also faced problems getting to the restricted "airside" via security checkpoints. As well as being delayed getting through security, many staff were also unfamiliar with the building and systems they were using. Many workers had not been familiarised with the new terminal and that many "didn't know where to go, what bags to get".

It took an hour for people to get to the right place. One said, "The place is so enormous, we don't know where we are going, we've been given no maps, no numbers to ring." Other staff reported that, due to poor morale, many had not attended training courses and trial runs. It was also claimed there were not enough people working at T5 on opening day. Once staff working that morning were in position, some workers in the baggage sorting area reported not being able to log on to the computer system, while others struggled to use the Resource Management System (RMS), which allocates handlers to load or unload flights. But despite the confusion behind the scenes, check-in staff continued to add luggage to the system, which is designed to handle 12 000 bags an hour. This then led to "meltdown" with bags clogging up the underground conveyor system because baggage workers were not removing them quickly enough at the other end.

By Thursday lunchtime the cumulative effect of the staff problems meant BA had to cancel 20 flights. By about 17:00 GMT the airline was forced to suspend all hold luggage check-in to try to clear the backlog of bags. This meant passengers already at the airport had the choice of either flying with just hand luggage, getting an alternative flight or claiming a refund. By the end of T5's first traumatic day, a total of 34 flights had been cancelled and hundreds of passengers had been left stranded. By Saturday, BA said it had a backlog of at least 15 000 bags at Heathrow.

Negotiating Change Management and Variations

A variation is an agreement supported by consideration to alter some terms of the contract. There should be express terms in contracts which give the power instruct variations. In the absence of express terms in the contract the contractor may reject instructions for variations without giving rise to any legal consequences. Therefore, most contracts contain a clause to allow for variations to the work and required of the contractor. This normally relates to the performance of additional work or services. The contractor may be authorized to perform additional work and/or supply additional goods without a competitive process, provided that such additions come within the general scope of the work. In this situation, the contract manager may need to negotiate with the contractor regarding costs, time and quality. This is a challenge given the incumbent contractor will know they are in a powerful position.

Variations in Contract Terms

Negotiating Variations is a key responsibility of the contract manager and the End User section, there are many potential sources of variations to the original scope or contract. These can include:

- Duration, effective and expiry dates
- Cost of additional service or works

- Price variations
- Extension of contract duration
- New scope of work and terms
- Price Variations

Often the variations related to actual increases or decreases in material, labour, commodity or energy and fuel costs or links to specified indices relevant to supply market costs, such as commodity price indices and labour market indices. In these cases, prices will be allowed to increase or decrease in line with market conditions.

The Variation Process

When the variation is at the request of the client, then a variation document prepared by client and signed by client and the contractor to introduce changes to the terms, conditions, or activities of an existing contract. The business case for the variation will need to include:

- Duration, effective and expiry dates
- Contract value including pervious Variation Orders
- Total expenditure and outstanding commitment to-date.
- Objectives
- Define the objective:
- Extension of contract duration
- New scope of work / terms
- Additional funds
- Justification for change
- Considered alternatives
- Provide existing rates/ changed rates
- Recommendation and Budget
- Recommended duration of contract extension, if any
- Changes in scope and revised contract value
- Anticipation of further extension(s), if any

It is the responsibility of the End-User to initiate the Variation Order by issuing a "memorandum" with the above details and the End-User needs to obtain approvals in accordance with the organisations tendering procedures.

In the event of the variation coming from the contractor, then the End-User will screen the request for technical justification and assess the price in partnership with contracting section and obtain the necessary approval in accordance with tendering procedures. The financial authority levels for approving Variation Orders is governed by the provisions of the Financial Authorities. The End-User is responsible for obtaining these approvals. A series of Variation Orders must be viewed cumulatively, once the total value of all variations is reaches 20% of the original contract value then the contract manager needs to seek approval of senior management to proceed. This is part of good governance and prevents scope creep and projects going out of control. Variation Orders with no monetary value still need to be reviewed by senior management. The contracting section needs to determine whether any proposed Variation Order introduces "significant changes" to the contract terms and the legal and contractual implications.

Service Level Agreements

The Service Level Agreement (SLA) Is a contract between a service provider and the end user (or the internal customer) that defines the level of service expected from the service provider. SLAs are output-based in that their purpose is specifically to define what the customer will receive. It is very important the terms of the SLA are agreed during the contract commercial negotiation stage and not imposed after the agreement is signed.

The Service Level Agreement Document

The SLA needs to contain several crucial elements to ensure that the level of service agreed during the commercial negotiation is provided by the contractor, these include:

- The business objectives to be achieved in the provision of the services, this is to ensure that the SLA deliverables support the objectives and overall ethos of the organisation.
- It will describe in detail the service deliverables in terms of specific and detailed Key Performance Indicators.
- It will clearly define the performance standards the customer expects in the provision of the services by the service provider, these need to reflect what was agreed during the commercial negotiation phase of the process.
- It will provide an ongoing reporting mechanism for measuring the expected performance standards, this will be framed around the KPIs and will monitored and fed back by the customer and used by the contract manager to manage the contract and the contractor.
- It will provide a remedial mechanism and compensation regime where performance standards are not achieved, whilst incentivising the service provider to maintain a high level of performance. The client will therefore

be entitled to some form of refund or credit for non-performance, but this must be a balance between sufficient to motivate the provide to improve, but not harsh enough to create a adversarial reaction.

- It will provide a mechanism for review and change to the service levels over the course of the contract. As the contract rolls out there may well be changing circumstances that need to be reflected in revised SLA and KPI
- Ultimately the SLA will give the customer the right to terminate the contract where performance standards fall consistently below an acceptable level, over a period. Without this option, there is little to ensure providers consistent delivery of service.

Calculating and Negotiating Service Credits

The service credit is a percentage rebate from service charges, for each percentage point that service provision falls short of the agreed service standard. The accumulation of service credit 'points' across a range of service level measures, which are then periodically converted into credits based on a formula. The contract manager may use the 'multiplier' mechanisms to impose extra service credits for problems that re-occur within specified timescales. These may need to be negotiated with the provider, especially if the KPI have not been clearly set out and agreed in the SLA.

Gainshare Contracts

The contract manager may need to negotiate the implementation of gainshare agreements.

- Negotiating what is "expected" service and what is a "super" service
- Defining cause and effect
- Dealing with the effect of events outside the supplier's control
- Determining the amount of risk / reward – usually a % of price – and how long

Negotiation of Claims

A claim is a request made by one party to a contract for relief or compensation to remedy certain damages or to cover costs incurred by the claimant because of the other party's default or due to unforeseen adverse circumstances. There are two types of claims Contractual and non-contractual. In most situations, non-contractual claims (or sympathy payments) are rejected. The contractual claim must be in writing and presented within a reasonable period of time (60 days is typical).

In terms of commercial negotiation, the contract manager needs to maintain the claim narrative, and therefore be well prepared, so that they can negotiate effectively with contractors. The contract manager may have to dispute the value of the claim and negotiate a mutually acceptable figure. Often this narrative is missing and that can affect the outcome of the commercial negotiations.

Typical Claims
What can be claimed for by the contractor is contained in the original contractual terms and conditions, these can include:

- Increased labour, plant and site establishment
- Damage to plant and equipment
- Disruption and productivity losses due to actions of the client
- Extra site visits as requested by the client
- Head Office overheads
- Financing of late payments when client fails to meet agreed payment terms

Supplier Relationship Management (SRM)

The primary aim of Supplier Relationship Management is the creation and maintenance of strategic relationships, this will often involve in the contract manager in commercial negotiations to resolve issues and progress the project. In the case of high strategic value relationships which are implicitly linked with business success and competitive advantage, commercial negotiations need to reflect that importance. Suppliers can be categorised under three general headings:

- Strategic suppliers are the smallest tranche, representing only about 5%
- Tactical, or core, suppliers, constituting approximately 15% of the total
- Transactional suppliers normally represent the majority at 80%

Factors that Affect the Relationship
There are many factors that can affect the nature and the quality of the relationship between the contract manager and the provider. In situations where issues arise, they may need to be resolved making use of appropriate forms of commercial negotiation.

There is a lack of trust between the parties involved
Where there is an obvious lack of trust between the two parties, this can be improved by more open and transparent communications, regular meetings and

principled style commercial negotiations with the supplier. The contract manager may need to investigate the root cause of this miss trust, it may be historical and or anecdotal and not borne out by current events. A lack of trust will greatly inhibit the agile and collaborative management of contracts and therefore these issues need to be negotiated and resolved.

There is a low degree of transparency between the parties
Regular round table meetings and win/win style commercial negotiations can improve transparency. Focus group events and clear and appropriate channels of communication between both sides are very important.

Neither (or only one side) feel that they are gaining mutual commercial benefit from the contract
The contract manager will need review of contractors estimated to actual costs. This may indicate that the contractor is facing reduced margins and prices may need to be renegotiated. The contract manager may need to benchmark contractor prices more frequently to ensure VFM and increase the sense of confidence in the commercial benefit being derived and if not, then a new negotiation may need to take place.

Both (or one side) fail to keep their commercial promises
Failure to keep respective commercial promises may be due to operational and or financial restrictions placed upon one or both sides. There may be a need to negotiate and/or re define the commercial expectations of both parties. There is always the risk of over promising and under delivering during commercial negotiations.

Neither (or only one side) wants to share the risks
Often contract terms and conditions are designed to pass liability and risk onto the other party. This can lead to protracted and positional win/lose style commercial negotiations which inhibit agile and collaborative working. Both sides need to consider risks as part of the cost of doing business and make full use of risk and value classifications tools to determine the type of risk, strategic or routine and its potential impact and probability and then negotiate a mutually acceptable risk management strategy.

Both sides fail to regard each other with mutual respect
A lack of respect, in terms of competency, skills, ability, and professionalism of either side can have a significant impact the quality of the relationship.

Conducting all commercial negotiations in a professional and principled way can help to build that mutual respect and trust.

All Payment are made to terms

One of the most significant impacts upon relationships is related to payment terms. Often contractors believe that stated payment terms of 30 days, actually means they can expect payment within 30 days. The reality is that the contract manager will often need to review invoices with stakeholders, seek or negotiate approval from absent/busy senior managers. It is important therefore to negotiate payment expectations from the client side and for contractors to understand the issues facing the contract manager regarding the internal processing of their invoices.

There are many cultural differences between the two organisations

Organisational cultural differences can affect strategic contracts significantly and should really have been identified at the Contractor selection stage. Both sides need to understand the relative cultures of their respective organisations when conducting commercial negotiations. This often the case when public and private sector organisations are involved. The contractor will be driven by business development, profit, and shareholder value, whereas the public sector is focussed on value for money and social good.

There is a 'blame culture' between the contract manager and the provider

"Blame" is often a feature of poorly drafted scopes of work and adversarial terms and conditions that where negotiated prior to handover. In this scenario, both sides will seek to allocated blame for non-performance. In this scenario, both sides need to focus on the root cause of the issues and address them together and negotiate a mutually acceptable solution. It must be remembered that the blame game and win/lose style commercial negotiations are time consuming, counter-productive and damaging to any commercial relationships and rarely leads to a sustainable solution.

There is a low degree of empowerment on the part of those who manage the relationship

A lack of empowerment from both sides can greatly inhabit the ability to negotiate effectively. Both sides need to be agile and work collaboratively. Senior management may need to review the internal structures and levels of delegated authorities, to enable both sides to negotiate sensible and well-judged commercial decisions to ensure mutually beneficial outcomes.

Failure to invest in training and development

Both organisations need to invest in training and development for their respective relationship managers. Failure to so will lead to a steady decline in commercial performance. The commercial negotiation training requirements of both sides need to be review, taking full account of the skills, knowledge and competencies need to manage agile and collaborative contractual relationships. Professional bodies like IACCM have a suite of training courses designed to enable and empower contract managers.

Post Award Contract Management and Administration

Definition
"Best Practices Contract management is a process by which a contractor is motivated and enabled to achieve extra value added, over and above that which has been specified originally and assessable against criteria in the original contract. The process should be to the benefit of both parties".

Contract Administration
The effective and efficient administration of contracts is critical to the overall success of any contract. The process can include many the activities for example maintaining signed copies of contracts and is an important part of the process. We need to have a process to ensure that key trigger points are recorded, and action taken, for example contract termination dates.

We also must have a process whereby regular reports and (indeed ad hoc reports) of transactions, issues, events etc are produced as management information and distributed to appropriate stakeholders in the process of contract management. Contract administration is key to a successful contract close out, whereby the lessons learned from contract execution can be disseminated throughout the organisation.

It is critical that the value secured by the contracting and negotiation process is not allowed to leak out due to the poor management of contracts post-award.

Chapter Summary
In this chapter we have considered:

* The process of transition and implementation of negotiated agreements and contracts
* The negotiation of contractual and operational variations
* The negotiation of claims
* How to maintain the relationship and still negotiate to secure objectives and VFM

- The negotiation of revised KPIs and SLAs
- The overall process of management of the contract, post-award

---

Case Study

Torch Consultants are a group of procurement consultants, based in London. The company has recently secured a contract for the supply of a team of consultants to assist in the development of a scope of work for the new gas plant turnkey contract for Allied Oil and Gas plc. Part of the contract includes attending a series of meetings with the key stakeholders at the various sites around the UK. These are considered very important events. Up to date the consultants have missed a number of these events. A meeting is planned for the 15th July at 10am. Two consultants from Torch are due to attend. By chance, this meeting will also be attended by the CEO of Allied – Ms Alison Dacha.

Due to a family crisis, one consultant does not make the meeting and the other one is late by one hour, due to local traffic. Alison is very angry at this unprofessional behaviour and informs the consultants that she intends to terminate the whole contract, with immediate effect and will make a claim for his wasted time, given that this critical event has not been properly resourced by Torch. The consultants have requested a meeting to discuss the situation.

Task

As the consultants, what actions would you suggest to Alison to try and get this project back on track?

Author Biographies

Dr Ray Carter MA, MCIPS, MCMI, Cert Ed. UK Licensed Paralegal. Author of "Practical Procurement" and "Practical Contact Management" and creator of the 10 (C) model. CIPS UK Services Index Panel Member.
Ray is an international training and development consultant. He began his management career in the public sector and thereafter for a large food manufacturer in the UK. He graduated from University with a Master's degree in Management Studies. Ray is also a licenced contract management paralegal.

His first book relating to supply chain management entitled *Integrated Materials Management*, was published in 1982 by Pearson and has become a recommended text for a number of courses, including the Chartered Institute of Purchasing and Supply. This was followed by *Stores and Distribution Management*, published by Liverpool Academic Press in 2005. *Practical Procurement* (with Steve Kirby and Paul Jackson) was published by Cambridge Academic and was followed by *Practical Contract Management*, the second edition of which was published by Cambridge Academic in 2018.

Ray has had numerous articles and papers published in journals such as *Supply Management* and the Centre for Advanced Procurement's *Praxis* publication. Ray's now famous '10c's' of supplier evaluation model, first published in 1995, has now become an accepted model for the evaluation of supplies and contractors and has been adopted by many organisations. It is also now part of the CIPS level 4 syllabuses and IACCM Practitioner level programs.

Until 1991 Ray was Principal Lecturer in Supply Chain Management at the Business School, University of North London. In recent years, he has undertaken training and consultancy assignments for organisations such as Virgin Media, Boots, Serco, Rolls Royce, Oracle, East Tames Housing, European Patent Office, Total Oil, RBS, Shell, East Lothian Council, Lucas Engineering and Systems, the Chartered Institute of Purchasing and Supply, BRC, Nederlandse Aardolie Maatschappij.B.V, Abu Dhabi Company for Onshore Oil Operations NDC, ADNOC, UK Intervention Board, Ericsson, Bradford City Council, British Aerospace, Marconi, BBC, Magnox, Ordnance Survey, Chevron USA, Caspian Pipeline Consortium, Tengzichevroil Company, Medway Council, Coca-Cola and Shell International BV.

Ray has worked in many locations, including the Far East, the Middle East, South America, Europe and Africa. Most of these events have been related to strategic issues in relation to supply chain management, procurement and contracting.

Kenny Campbell MCIPS, CCMP

Kenny is a Training Consultant for DPSS Consultants (Developing People Serving the Supply Chain) which is an international training and development consultancy comprising of 25 specialist consultants. Kenny's personal vision is to design and to deliver training that is memorable, fun and engages the learner to bring about behaviour change. Kenny has 25 years of training and development experience working in large blue-chip organisations and as a freelance consultant.

Kenny began his procurement career with BT Procurement in Edinburgh before being recruited to BT's Procurement Training organisation in 1989. As part of the Procurement Training team in BT Kenny was responsible for design and delivery of a range of functional training courses for BT buyers on indirect and direct procurement. During this time BT Procurement won the Chartered Institute of Purchasing and Supply (CIPS) "Purchasing department of the year" award.

Having completed the Professional exams of the CIPS in 1995 he became involved in the delivery of the BT / CIPS Distance learning scheme at Foundation and Professional level. This involved working to design workshops and run revision weekends with delegates for the full range of CIPs subjects including Logistics, Tactics and Operations, Legal Aspects and Strategy. These courses at postgraduate level gave Kenny a great overview of the whole supply process from identification of need through Strategic analysis, to more detailed contract management and indirect procurement. As part of a joint venture between BT/Accenture, Kenny moved to e-peopleserve in 2000 and subsequently to Accenture HR services extending his portfolio into Leadership, Performance Management and Interpersonal skills training.

Since 2002 Kenny has worked as an independent training consultant for a range of clients either directly or with trusted partners such as DPSS Consultants, International Association of Contract and Commercial Management (IACCM), Horizon Associates, PODA, BrayLeino Broadskill, Knowledge Pool and Blue Highways Services.

In recent years he has undertaken assignments for organisations in a wide variety of sectors from Manufacturing to Government including Thames Water, Siemens, Chevron, Total, National Grid, Accenture, UK Prison Service, Thales, Experian, Foreign and Commonwealth Office and Tanzanian Telecomms Regulatory Authority. The events delivered have covered a wide range of topics including, Influencing, Negotiation, Direct and Indirect Procurement, Supply Chain Management, Leadership, Strategy Compliance and Coaching.

Based in the UK, Kenny is comfortable working in a variety of locations, having completed assignments in Nigeria, Angola, Indonesia and the Netherlands. He recently undertook his CCMA qualification with IACCM.

INDEX